16 Manor Way

I0118162

The Story of Our Fated Adoptions

Nicholas Holbrook

chipmunkapublishing
the mental health publisher

Nicholas Holbrook

Published by
Chipmunkapublishing
PO Box 6872
Brentwood
Essex CM13 1ZT
United Kingdom

http://www.chipmunkapublishing.com

Chipmunkapublishing gratefully acknowledge the support of Arts Council England.

Prologue

Smilingly happy on the outside, but inside so very confused

It was at Reading railway station that it came to me in a moment of clarity how I should begin our story. Reading of all places eh? I don't go there very often but on this occasion I was travelling back on my own after we had spent the Bank Holiday weekend down in Somerset with my wife's parents Jan and Tony.

Being the Bank Holiday, it was of course raining.

Reading is never the most attractive of places even on a beautiful day, despite all of the imaginative new architecture that is going up each and every month. However, it looked particularly drab and somehow rather northern on this particular wet day. The water streamed off the station roof filling pools on Platform 4, water that simply couldn't drain away, and so the pools just got larger. Each time that someone walked along the platform to get onto our train, they had to walk just that little bit further round the expanding puddle than the last person had. Another ten minutes of heavy rain and no-one else could have reached the train. The South West Trains staff just looked at the scene of course. There was no thought in their heads of taking out a broom and sweeping away the water to help their already damp passengers. No way.

"Welcome to Platform 4, welcome to Reading, you're in the UK now mate."

"Not my job, mate, the second shift can take care of that!"

I don't suppose that they ever did. I reckon that puddle just kept on getting bigger and deeper throughout the afternoon. It's probably still there, on Platform 4, let me know when you're next in Reading on a wet afternoon, will you?

I watched some very different people getting onto our train. A group of noisy men boarded not long after I had. Seven of them I think. Very boisterous and confident, they sounded threatening for a moment as they entered my section. I didn't like it. However, when some of them came into view further down the carriage, I could see clearly that they were in their late twenties or early thirties, and they sounded like they have been away to a sports event of some kind. They were probably not the threat to me that my mind had first assumed. Just some English lads being lads.

Next, a group of large and oh so badly-dressed Americans waddled up the platform towards the carriages at the front of the train, pulling their flimsy waterproof jackets tightly about them as the platform's roof-cover ended, braving the last few yards out and into the miserable Reading rain. One of the men in their group had on some very smart tan suede shoes, perhaps he was their tour leader. Just maybe, when their group was lost, instead of looking for their guide waiving an umbrella shouting weakly: "My group this way, now stick together folks, after all you don't want to get lost round here everyone's a Muslim you know!"

maybe they just looked down at the ground for the reassuring sight of his very distinctive shoes. He deftly stepped round the puddle I noticed, keeping his splendid footwear completely dry and dirt-free. Wouldn't want to got them wet now would you?
I reckon he must have been wearing them for the first time that very day.

"Nice blouson too, my American friend. Nice to see you all here, really. Thanks for making the trip, we do appreciate you flying over the pond."

A young lady, wearing shockingly pink and white clothes, came in and sat down opposite me, and did do very purposefully. You were not going to miss seeing her, believe me. With terrific vigour she shook the rain off her dazzling white raincoat, and stamped her pristine white sports shoes on the floor of the carriage, and again looked at me, annoyingly. I wasn't sitting

4

there with my feet up on the seat or anything immoral like that. I didn't smell, as far as I knew, and I had no reason to believe that my looks were that offensive to fellow travellers, or that my posture was especially bad that wet afternoon. I concluded that she was looking at me disapprovingly for a very more simple reason, namely my clothes. My theory, rapidly reached, was that she didn't like the colour! I was wearing jeans and my Barbour fishing fleece that Dad and I had bought some years ago together up in Farlows in Pall Mall. That would have been the last time that my father and I had gone shopping together, for sure. Of all the colours in the world, of all the possible shades and hues of fleece that this unfortunate young lady was forced to countenance this wet Sunday afternoon, I was sitting there directly opposite "Miss Pink and White 2007" wearing a Barbour fleece in yes agricultural brown! Ugh!! Oh, how ever did she manage, it must have been dreadful for her? She looked really put out. I moved to the seat on the other side of the carriage, such was her indignation at my brownness. I was tired and I was thinking of bigger things, none of them pink or indeed white I'm afraid, Miss. Things that were of more significance to me, Nick.

I carry sadness with me every day, and it works away on my mind every hour of every day. When I'm awake, and also when I'm asleep. I know that because I have vivid dreams. Interesting word "vivid" isn't it? It often seems to accompany the noun "dreams". That girl's clothes, they were pretty vivid. Anyway, I should probably have had some counselling over twenty years ago after Mum's suicide, but I didn't. We didn't. Lots of things that should have happened in our family didn't, and usually it was the very big things. The biggest ones in fact. The things that actually most needed doing that had the greatest need and the greatest pain and the greatest history and the greatest urgency behind them, but they just plain and simply didn't get done. I think the problem was that our parents just didn't see how important and big these things were and how they needed addressing in order for Claire and I to have any decent chance of coming through what we went through in any kind of reasonable shape. Such important things just weren't seen, they certainly weren't understood and above they all definitely didn't get addressed. They just didn't acted on, when they needed to.

But they should have.

Period.

On this Bank holiday, as I sat there on my South West Trains service from Reading to London Waterloo, (I was getting off at Ascot, it's pronounced "Ascut" so you know), a thought came to me very clearly. I said it was the thought that I wanted to begin this book with you may remember. It felt very natural and comfortable as an idea just sitting there in my mind, and it was the kind of idea that enters your head with such a simple approach and at such a natural pace, that I really did wonder why I had never thought this particular thought before. Miss Pink and White across the way there in the train carriage might have noticed a slight smiling upturn on my lips at that precise moment.

I really might have had this notion before. It must be me, perhaps I am really plain slow.
So, here was the thought that I had that damp May Sunday, and I want to share it with you because it is so just so pure. The thought that came into my head and stayed was this:

It could all have been so different. Just that, that was it.

Profoundly different in fact. I mean us, our family, what we went through, what happened to all four of us. With just a little more standing up for Claire and I, for just a little more attention to those "crucial conversations" that were screeching out to be had, with just a little more imagination, and most importantly with a little more Love, our lives could have been so very different, to this very day.

Radically different in fact, and without the pain.

Now that would have been nice.

16 Manor Way

A tiny change in direction was all that was required to get us all to a very different place from the one that we find ourselves in now. In fact, we need never have known about the place where we did actually get to, the place that we did journey to that is so very full of great sadness and personal tragedy for our family. All darkness. Yet, it could all have been so completely different, really. And more bearable.

At 13.42, we slowly left behind the substantial puddle on Platform 4 and our blue, white and red train pulled out into the Reading grey.

What do you think it is that makes one member of a family outlive all of the others? I wonder what power decided that I was going to outlive Mum, that I would outlive Dad and now dear Claire too? This was not my choice, this was not my plan.

Our first stop was to be at Winnersh Triangle.

This is a question that I can't answer, I simply don't know. However, the one thing of which I am completely certain is that I will tell the story of what happened to my family, as the survivor from that little group. In my mid-forties, it has become overwhelmingly important to me to write this book. I am quite sure that the regular bad dreams that I have of my family and what we experienced, are happening in my head even now because I experience a powerful need to write the story down. They wake this troubled grown man up, and frequently, while my family sleeps peacefully about me. I need to get our story out of my head and onto paper before it gets lost. I believe that the intensity and the frequency of my dreams are both there for a reason, to drive me on to getting our family story written down. I really believe that this is true.

From reading our family story, I invite you to decide if you think we ever were a real family. You should make up your own mind on this. I have two opposing views flying round my head. We most definitely lived together in the same house for nearly nineteen years so yes we were a family in that sense. We went about our daily family business, seemingly much like any other family and we were seen by others doing this just like they did with their own family. No apparent difference, no visible variation on the theme.

"So, everything must be okay with them then, mustn't it?" our neighbours must have all thought.

"No difference that we can see, nope, not there, not at No.16 Manor Way!
All quiet there, really. We don't notice anything unusual or out of place happening behind that solid, wooden front door, painted in elegant claret. I think all must be well. Now, where did I put that paper I was about to read….?"

Letters and Christmas cards would come addressed to "The Holbrooks" or to "Dr and Mrs Holbrook & family". There you are you see, it was official, we were a family, the Post Office said so! Or the "GPO" or General Post Office as it was called in those days.

"You are a family, it's here printed in black and white ink on gazillions of envelopes that were put through the tightly-hinged brass post-flap on the door of 16 Manor Way over the years."

I guess that we always thought of ourselves as a family, but the question that is now so often in my head is "Were we a true family?" After all, the four of us were thrown together by wildly random circumstance, we had come from four different sources and we know that none of us was blood-related to any of the others. Now there's a significant variation for starters! Open your eyes Manor Way neighbours, there's one that you missed already! You were so near to the Holbrooks, yet so very, very far, and it happened right under your noses.

You missed it folks.
You made assumptions, big ones.
You all judged the book by its cover.

16 Manor Way

We had hugely different backgrounds you see, completely different personalities and very different talents. DNA totally different x four. Tragically, some also had demons to fight, as you will read. Perhaps we all had.

I want you to know that I have written this book for two specific reasons. The first is that I know deep inside in my heart that there is a story needing to be told. It is completely proper and reasonable that it be recorded in writing, the story of The Holbrooks as we were known.

I believe that it's a very powerful story too. I have to remind myself of that fact quite firmly as of course it doesn't always seem that way to me. Nothing really seems that extraordinary to you if you're very closely involved with it, now does it? It's what you went through so it must be normal, right? Well, actually no.

I have only to take a few very brief moments to stand back from the family that was the Holbrooks in 16 Manor Way, Blackheath, London SE3 9EF, for me to see true privilege, joy, love, tragedy and enduring pain, pain that I feel more than ever today. Ours is indeed a powerful story. My challenge is to tell it in full. I like to think that Claire would have wanted that too. And I should also try to tell it sufficiently well that you can understand it as the reader. I hope that I have done that for you pretty well.

By definition, all of our experience is ordinary as far as we are concerned isn't it? It's something that you're entirely used to, so how can anything that "little old me" went through ever really be extraordinary or powerful or significant or of interest to others?

Well, maybe it can, and I think the story of our family may do exactly that.

The second reason is more important to me. I want this book and the story that it tries to tell to shout out from the page as loudly as it is possible, the sadness that comes into your life when a loved one suffers so painfully from a creeping illness that we call Alcoholism. A lethal one too.

I want my pages to shout out too the numbness and the guilt and the fictional shock (because it can't be real), that hurts you so dreadfully when someone you think you know or love, kills themselves. When they take their own life away, and suddenly so. Without any warning. At all.

To shout out about the stunning impact that crashes into you when your remaining parent suddenly re-marries and handles it as badly as it is humanly possible to handle it.

To shout out about the irreversible damage that is done when over twenty years of fabulous, fabulous, fabulous, relationships are smashed to smithereens in a series of mere moments, moments that it turns out may never, ever be reversed, under any circumstances.

"Oh, never?" "No, never."

No-one ever came to help my sister Claire and I, no-one followed up on us after what we went through, as far as I know to this day. Not one single competent professional person thought to provide us with any counselling of any kind to help us to adjust, even a little, perhaps to talk, to discuss, to open up, to grieve, to share, to begin to cope, to begin to understand that others have gone through this too, to know what the hell it was that had just hit us. Not even you Dad and you should have done that more than anyone else, not just as our father, but as a Medical man. I sometimes think that I must have done something really bad in a former existence to have gone though this and not had that support from the man that we called Dad. Maybe I did?

I am quite sure that no-one other than Claire and I knew how much deep hurt and freezing sadness and pain and anger and bitterness and bile we carried in our heart as a result of what we went through. That's why I want this story to be told, as best as I am able. It's too bad that these things happen at all, but it's even worse that they then get repeated. You can tell that I am angry and that I am bitter. The fact is that these feelings take something out of every single day of my life, even twenty five years later, and I don't see how they will ever really stop doing that.

I know that they did the same to Claire too, but I failed to have the imagination to see this in time. I was too busy feeling sorry for myself, and meanwhile she was on her own.

Through circumstance.

Yes, you are right, of course I'm angry, you can see that plainly, but more importantly, I'm also passionate. I tell this story "for the record". According to a search on the web, there are approximately 6 billion people on this planet. There is now only one of them who knows this particular story, that's just one person in 6 billion. A very small percentage, whatever the figure is.

How often must that be repeated all over our planet? If I don't tell it, no-one else will. It would die with me. Quite simply, no-one else knows it now, not from the inside. No-one else can tell it. Oh sure, some people know bits of it, and some people know some bits that I don't know, but no-one who is still alive today has lived through this, other than me.

And so I choose to tell it.

To be the teller of our story.

To deliver some writings.

To play the part of Messenger.

Stay with this book please if you're interested in **families**.

Stay with this book if you have an interest in **relationships**.

Certainly stay here if **love of other people** is important to you.

If the subject of **adoption** is significant for you in any way, stay with me.

If you have been affected by **alcoholism** in any way, you should read this.

If anyone in your family, or circle of friends, colleagues or neighbours, has **committed suicide**, then you will want to hear the story of the Holbrook family. I guess that might be painful, but then you know this already. I know it too, very well. Claire and I started knowing this when we were younger than was perhaps fair.

I know that many people go through far more than my sister and I did. I do know that.
I know that a very tiny number of people go through far worse still, and that they witness things that they never should have to see. At the time of my writing this, we have been shown distressing scenes in America following the devastation caused by Hurricane Katrina only recently.

If you allow it to, the television news will confirm for you daily that tragedy happens only too frequently and is shown to us on our television screens, and in colour, while selfishly we send text messages on our phones, sip decaf latte coffee, and order our takeaway meal, all in time for Britain's Got Talent, the semi-final, beginning at 8.30 pm.

So this book is not about scoring points, - emphatically not. It's not about comparing my family's sadness to another's, in any way at all. Nor is it about me saying that the suffering that we went through, and still go through, around Mum's drinking for example was identical to, or any worse than, what another person went through in their relationship. Or that my Dad getting re-married was worse than what you may have gone through when one of your parents did that too. I understand by now that being a human amongst other humans doesn't work that way. I have learnt a little.

In case it needs to be said I'm not asking for pity either by the way. I'll get on with my life as best as I can, I'm confident I've always done that pretty well. With a mask on, but getting on with things. Surface, sub-surface.

As I record our story here I would guess that you may relate to a part of it, or maybe to more than one part. The sheer amount of raw human experience that has been thrust upon my family means that the story of the Holbrook family will definitely have parallels in some readers' lives, at least I think it very likely.

Writing it down, and getting some of it out of my head, may also help me to let go, something needs to achieve that. I suspect that it's all burned too deeply into me for me to ever let go really. It's so much part of me that it has shaped me psychologically I'm fully sure, and I don't think that I can really undo that.

Can we ever? Should we? There again, maybe we're the stronger for it.

It is a true story, to the very best of my knowledge. I make that commitment to you. Actually I will go further that that and link here and now my personal integrity to it. If I have written in this book, or have made a comment, in a way that I know is not true and which I know is completely inaccurate, ...well you understand what I'm saying.
That's my integrity gone in a moment, but I'm not planning to allow this to happen. The intangible thing called integrity matters greatly to me. I place a value on it.

It is a story that is strongly connected to the 1960s and the 1970s in particular and indeed to the very early 1980s too. It's a story of its time definitely, yet paradoxically it could also happen at any time, and probably does. You'll see what I mean very soon.

I tell it as best I can, I have tried to bring it to life to the best of my ability and I strive to get it out of my head (and other's who have helped) so that you can read it.

Enjoy it if you can. Get goodness from it if you can. I'd simply love it if you can get strength from it, now wouldn't that be a wonderful result for us both? Perhaps then some of the pain and the crying late at night and the waking from dreams in the early hours might have a little reason.

I have tried to tell parts of it as though we are both watching a scene, and I hope that I've given it some life.

Funny that isn't it, giving life to so many dead and dying things?

Adoption:

Depression:

Alcoholism:

Next, suicide:

The destruction of a family:

Parkinson's:

Meningitis:

Our family….

16 Manor Way

I thank you for reading our story, for reading about what went on behind the solid wooden door of 16 Manor Way, where the Holbrooks lived. Here's what happened.

Nicholas Holbrook

Chapter 1 – the 1960s & Our Adoption

Fortunate in Adoption, but with roots more humble

Long before I was born in 1961, something happened that continues to have an almighty effect on my life today. It was something that occurred I would guess probably around 1936, and it would have happened to our Mum. Somewhere in the Stockton-on-Tees area. I can't say more, I know no more. I am not even one hundred per cent sure that it did in fact happen. It's rather like the comet hitting the planet and wiping out the dinosaurs, things do seem to point to it having happened, but where and when is less easy to pinpoint. "Show me the proof and I'll believe you".

That's the good news. The bad news is that I don't know what it was, or precisely when it was. I think I might sort of know, I do have some loose kind of an idea, but I can't be sure. I don't believe now that I ever will be either. I'll tell you what I think it was in a moment, but let me explain by starting at what was the beginning of this story for me, my birthday.

Young Nicholas was born in 1961, actually on January 5th 1961. Do you know someone who was born around that time? Perhaps you were yourself? Or a member of your immediate family maybe? I don't remember the experience myself, you'll understand that I was very young at the time! Believe me when I say that it's a "naff" time of year to have a birthday. It's just so near to Christmas that everyone forgets about it, and it was only when the Christmas period was over and done with that family friends would say (and they still do!) "When's your birthday then Nick, I know it's around now isn't it?" They used to ask me that around late January I seem to remember. Still, it could be worse, I might have had a birthday on December 24th or even on the 25th, something like that. That must be nice, but rather disorientating at the same time.

"Happy Christmas, oh and by the way, this is your Birthday present too!"

My sister's birthday was in June. Now there's a good time of year to have a birthday party! The 11th June Claire, Happy Birthday. Warm summer evenings in south London in the 60s and 70 s, how fondly I remember them as I look back.

So, the day when I was invited so kindly to live on our wonderful planet is well over forty years ago now. It would have been sixteen years after the Second World War had ended. That would have been a very different time to today. Clearly I can't remember the early 1960s for reasons that I don't think I need to state, but I am very pleased and actually a little proud to say that I do have good and clear memories of the late 1960s, some at least. I remember vividly a family friend of ours Mary taking me for a walk one day in Blackheath in south London, somewhere around 1966. It must have been a cold day as I was particularly well-wrapped up, in a thick grey coat and blue woollen hat. I remember clearly the railway bridge that we had just walked across that afternoon, and seeing the train going right underneath where we were standing, seeing it slipping confidently into a tunnel leading to Kidbrooke. It was that lovely time of day in the late Autumn when it's starting to get very cold, the light is still there but it too is starting to fade steadily, and you can begin to look forward to going home for tea and toast, which Mary and I may well have done that very afternoon. I would have been about five years old then, and I remember this scene very clearly.

Mary would have been in her fifties, she took me to London Zoo one day too and bought me a real lion cub, but this particular one didn't take too much looking after as he came from the toy shop there.

Ah yes the 60s, the swinging 60s. I think that word might mean something very different these days to what was meant then! I remember being told how language is a changing thing. Not too much traffic on the roads then I guess. Fewer planes in the sky, less British people travelling on package holidays to Spain, no computers (worth talking about), no Internet, no iPod music players, no such things invented then as the mobile phone, no videos, digital cameras, DVD s or music centres. What TV there was would have been black and white only. Many houses were without carpets throughout and most had no central heating, many would have been built with outside toilets too.

"Oh'Er missus", not good in the middle of a winter's night when you needed to go, eh?!

Men would have got the train to work in the morning from Blackheath station, wearing sober grey suits, almost certainly with a plain crisp white shirt, sober dark-coloured tie and well-polished black shoes, always carrying the day's newspaper with them tucked under their arm, an umbrella in the other

"Just in case, you never know, it does look a little grey that way".

So this would have been a period of gradual recovery after the second World War, a time of some prosperity and liberalism too, and amazingly a time when Man was going to walk on the moon. Or at least that's what they wanted us all to think.

So, what must it have been like for a single woman to fall pregnant in the 1960s? For that's what happened to Charlotte, my natural mother.

What must it have been like? Consider that for a moment, if you will.

Oh.

What would have gone through her head? I believe that she was in her early twenties, and unmarried in 1960s Britain. Or indeed what might have gone through the heads of others around her?

Who could you talk to about it?

Where did you go?

Just what were your options?

Consider for a few moments what ideas and judgements would go through the heads of those other people, whoever they were. Family, friends, neighbours …

What would people say when they found out? Oh, the shame of it all…

"She did what? When? No, surely not, but they're a nice family. I've seen him walking to the station in the morning, sober grey suit, daily newspaper, umbrella, just in case, you never know…"

Not every family stood together under such circumstances. For some it was too much in 1960s Britain. Some families could not be guaranteed to have stood by you and supported you as their daughter. In 2007, I for one just can not imagine saying to our own daughter

"Go! Leave this house for you have brought shame on your family".

Yet we know that words just like those were spoken on occasions inside a family when a young single daughter became pregnant. In 1960s Britain. It happened, believe it.

Consider the power of the neighbours' twitching white lace curtains.

Feel the power of public disgrace.

See the legacy of a few moments' passion.

Imagine the strains, the clash of loyalties, the conflicting passions and the perceived threat to a family's dignity. Consider the encompassing mores of the day, the importance of the standing of your family above all in the local community, the loving relationships of so many years that were tested so violently in those few shocked minutes.

Who must it have been hardest on?

The daughter?

The Mother?

Or the father?

I don't know all of the details around my natural mother's pregnancy, I'll tell you very shortly what I do know, but it's not a lot I'm afraid, at least for the moment. At the time of writing, I'm doing something to find out a little more about my birth mother with a very helpful lady in our Social Services department called Gill, and I'm a little hopeful that we'll make some good progress, some day. This is not a book about tracing my natural parents. There are some fine books that tell that kind of story better than I can. But in terms of this book's story, this is where I come in, growing inside a lady called Charlotte.

It seems absurd to say that "I've never met her", for she grew me inside her womb, I guess from around April 1960. She then gave birth to me in January the following year. That was at a place called Worksop, near Nottingham to be precise, - the Kilton Hospital.
I bet it was grey, possibly raining or about to rain, like that day on Platform 4 at Reading railway station. A good day to take an umbrella, just in case, you never know …

Was she on her own, and if not, who was there to hold her hand?

When did she take the decision to go ahead and have her baby?

Did she carry on going to work, did she wear loose-fitting clothes for some months to hide her pregnancy, or did she move away from the area nearer the date of the baby's birth, my birth?

How was my birth?

I could be wrong about the weather of course, but you can see how it might have been like that, on an early January night in Worksop, near the middle of England. Naff time of year to give me a birthday Charlotte… I wonder when yours is/was?

"But thank you Charlotte. I haven't yet had the chance to say that to you, face to face. I hope that I will soon one day, quite soon. Our own children Jack and Sophie wouldn't be here if it hadn't been for you making the hugely brave decision that you made then. I should explain, forgive me, that they're your grandchildren. Thank you, from us all.
They're completely wonderful, our children.

Did you think that of me back in Worksop in 1961 I ask myself?"

"By the way, my father was who exactly …? Can you tell me that?"

There you are, there's an example of someone else in my family affected by something that happened long ago, long before they were even born, which they have little if any awareness of today. Why should they? - let them enjoy their childhood. Cause and effect … there'll be time for them to learn all about that another day.

Maybe you had little choice at the time, I don't know the circumstances at all well, but you tell me all about it one day Charlotte will you… and thank you again for your sheer bravery in the very early 60s. I don't suppose that saying "It can't have been easy", does it justice in any way. You must have been strong, or people around you were. Both perhaps. I hope both.

It's a little strange, but I've had very few thoughts until quite recently about my natural father. I don't even know his name, only his occupation – Salesman. Of educational books, that he sold to schools. That's where he met Charlotte: you see my birth mother was a school secretary. And that's about it. Charlotte had been at the school herself as a pupil I learned. I also learned recently through Gill that it was a very good girls' private school, in Leicestershire. Good solid reputation locally I believe. So that's where I believe they met and events took their course in some way, after that. The value of a good educational establishment eh? Look what it did for me!

There must have come a point when she let go of me. Perhaps it was minutes after the birth, maybe seconds – was she even allowed to hold me, or to see me? Perhaps I was whisked away into the future. Did she even know my gender? I can't be sure. Or were we together for some hours and days after, I don't know. I was quite young at the time you understand.

I don't know. I don't know very much at all. So many questions and so few answers.

What goes through her head as she hands me over to a nurse?

"Make your way in the world little one, like we all have to do. I can't be with you". Probably nothing as calm as that I would guess.

She must have had fear, anxiety, pain, love (?), guilt, panic, exhaustion, all of these coursing through her at one and the same moment.

Or maybe none of these? Maybe she was just exhausted. I wonder if the midwife was a funny one, like Nurse Gladys Emmanuelle in Ronnie Barker's "Open All Hours"?!

"What do you say there Mr Barker? I'm sure she would have been, don't you? Gladys and Charlotte, in a hospital in the middle of England. I feel a whole new episode coming on! We'll call this one "The arrival of young Nicholas" shall we? I'm sure it would have been a good one, you and me Ronnie."

I'd like to think that my mother was sad to see me go at least, we'd been together for nine months hadn't we?

I wonder when our skin last touched, when she last saw me. When she last heard me cry as I was carried out through the double doors, to an uncertain life ahead.

Thanks for having me Charlotte, thanks "Mum".

Chapter 2 – Mum and Dad

Did I even know them like I thought I did?

Sometime after this, I went to a private Adoption home, whatever that means. Someone must have looked after me, fed me, changed me, cuddled me, (or maybe not), and seen to me in some way. No Pampers or Huggies in those days, just plain white Terry towelling nappies. I don't suppose they stayed white too long, not Persil-white anyway. "Dirt is Good", yeah right. Hard work washing those things I'm quite sure, we don't know how good we have it nowadays.

I'm not clear how long I was there. Maybe some months. I was definitely there a few weeks at least but I don't have any of the important details, as yet. Where did you go then Charlotte? What life did you go back to? So many questions and so few answers.

I'm sure it was nice at the adoption home. Noisy maybe too. I have often tried to imagine the building from the outside. What did it look like? Was there a sign on the wall letting you know what went on inside? What colour was the front door, although maybe you were shown in round the back. Did the neighbours know what the home was really for? Did it have a milkman, they must have needed milk for sure inside. Lots.

I wonder who picked me up when I cried … in Cot no.54?

At some point between the months of January and May of 1961, I was adopted by the two people who I will call Mum and Dad from now on in my story. They will always be my Mum and Dad, I know that I will never refer to anyone else with those names. Mum and Dad, just like yours. Except that I wasn't related to them, at least not by blood. That's all, other than that there was no difference at all. My Mum and my Dad, just like yours.

My Mum was called Audrey, and my Dad was Brian. Audrey and Brian Holbrook. They would have come by car to the adoption home to collect me. A nice stylish convertible I think, in ocean blue, with lots of 60s chrome on it, with a column gear-change and maybe a vinyl bench seat running right across the front, oh, and those big fish-fins at the back. I can imagine the scene can't you? Them pulling up in their car having driven up the M1, or maybe the A1 more likely as it was in those days.

I've sometimes wondered what their journey was like, the journey in which they went to collect their son for the first time? Did they drive up from Blackheath in South London to Nottingham in the day, and go back again? Or did they perhaps stay up there the night before in a hotel, or with some friends, and then drive back with me that day? What was the car I was in? I think it was the Zephyr that I know they did have, or it might have been a green Triumph Herald, not sure. Both of them classic cars of course. There, my very first car ride was in a classic car, not bad eh? Good start young Nick!

You'll get to ride in your lovely Citroen DS one day that you dream of so often, in cream with brown leather interior, but for now it will have to be a British classic that you start off in, okay?

Did they stop for coffee on the way, and drink it from those stylish 1960s very tall, clear glass coffee mugs that I can see in my mind?
A bit of Mod music in the background in the café maybe? That nice new boy Cliff Richard singing away in the background, that would have been before he and all of his friends went on their "summer holiday" together I guess.

Mother's Pride, the Daily Express, and Woodbines everywhere.

1960s Britain. Minis, Cortinas and "Rollers" for the fortunate few.

Mum would have looked very stylish I'm sure, like something out of a Norman Parkinson photo. You know the style in those days, three quarter length trousers, tight and nicely cut blouse with half sleeves, flat shoes, big sunglasses – Audrey Hepburn, Audrey Holbrook, same thing, both big stars to me.

Dad would have been in boot-cut trousers, probably in a shade of grey with dead trendy brown lace-up suede shoes. Two eye-holes only I think. Audrey Robinson a great, great friend to our family said Mum and Dad were very happy when I came along…. Well they would be wouldn't they? It was me after all, I'm special as an adopted baby. I'm different. Always have been, me.

Different, special, hesitant.

Still am, different, me, even now.

What did they think as they were driving up to meet me?

What thoughts were going through their heads?

Were they sure they were doing the right thing?

What did they say to each other? What would you say?

Did they feel nervous?

What was Charlotte thinking?

Where was Charlotte?

What thoughts were going through her head that day?

Who handed me over?

Who first held me, Mum or Dad?

Who first spoke with me?

Had they even seen me before?

What were the main news items on that morning?

Who was top of the league in the football?

What did a pint of beer cost?

Why me?

Why us?

Why the circumstance?

And so the story builds …

So over the years, knowing that you are adopted makes you a little different, or rather it makes you feel different. Well, so did lots of other things, as we came to find out over the passing years.

Some time after I was adopted, Mum and Dad adopted a second child, a baby girl. Her name was Claire (or Clare). I don't know exactly when she came along but I think it was probably about a year or so after I was adopted, some time towards the end of 1962. It wasn't to be a very long acquaintance, as my first sister was taken back by her natural mother after a short while. I guess there must have been a statuary period that allowed for this to happen, weeks, maybe just a few weeks or some months maybe?

What do you think would be appropriate here?

What did those good and all-knowing people making the legislation of the day think was right and fair and balanced and suitable, in 1960s Britain?

How good were the people who made these decisions? The people who went into offices and made families, and then clocked off for the day, and then went back home. Just how good were they?

What checks and balances were in place? And who checked the checkers?

Did they get it right all of the time? I think not.

Can you imagine what that must have been like for everyone concerned – the baby Clare herself, the adoptive parents who had taken this girl into their hearts and their home, and the birth mother who had been parted from her new child?

And that I believe was that, as far as I know. I know no more. I came by this tiny fragment of family history only from one winter's evening in 16 Manor Way. It happened quite by chance. It was very late one evening I seem to remember, I think I had either gone to bed or was in my bedroom working. I would have been about thirteen or fourteen. The good old public school education that I was going through then gave you a long and demanding sequence of hurdles to clear each term, and you simply had to stay on top of the schedule. Clear one hurdle and then prep for the next one, and the next, and then the next. I did lots of school work, - projects, essays with a minimum of two thousand and five hundred words, critical analyses, language translations, gargantuan amounts of Latin, French and Spanish vocabulary learning, continuous exam revision, past papers, likely future questions, mocks at both O, A and S level, and so on. No wonder I had little success with young women.

At some point on that dark evening, I must have heard Mum crying outside on the landing, just a few feet from my closed bedroom door. I think she must have been having a conversation already with Dad, because as soon as I went outside my room to see her, Dad came round too from their bedroom on my right, as though about to continue a discussion that was already underway.

Mum was really upset I remember, and I think she may have been drinking. I am very sorry Mum if I got that wrong. At some point through her tears, she said

"I was thinking about Clare ...." and continued to sob. And she didn't mean my sister.

Dad then went on to tell me something pretty extraordinary there and then, as he stood there with his arm partially around Mum in an effort to support her and calm her down. What he said next was completely extraordinary, in terms of one little family at least. I sensed his arm round Mum wasn't working. Can you see the scene?

So, there we were, all three of us standing closely in only a few square feet on this winter's night, on the first floor landing in a very confined space and Dad then explained this to me. That there had been a girl called Clare who "we had to give back.... and Audrey's very upset about it". Those were his exact words, I remember them very clearly. Stake my life on it.

He didn't give any more information. I don't remember Mum saying anything more, just continuing to cry. She was very upset, probably upset to the core looking back on it. I think she had loved her first daughter quite a lot.

So, guess what? I then went back into my room to carry on with my prep, once I had made sure that Mum was with Dad, and yes you've guessed it, we never ever discussed the subject again!! Not later that night, or at breakfast time the next morning, or a couple of days afterwards or over the following weekend – just plain common all-garden never. No wonder Sue says that I never face up to things or resolve open issues. How right you are Darling. WE NEVER DISCUSSED THE FACT THAT THERE HAD BEEN ANOTHER CHILD IN OUR FAMILY!! How unbelievable is that?

If this story was true, I can't imagine the sadness this must have caused everyone concerned, but particularly my Mum. She would have had two healthy children, one boy and one girl, and then had to hand one child back. How do you measure the pain of that? All that stuff I was just talking about when they came to collect me from cot No. 54, but in reverse. There would have been a moment when you handed back your child to someone, never to see them again. Now who got that business wrong, eh? One of those people sitting in an office making families I shouldn't wonder.

Actually, perhaps you can measure the associated sadness in the fact that when my sister was adopted sometime later in 1962, that's my "second" sister Claire who will always be my sister, my parents called my new sister exactly the same name, Claire! That's completely bizarre isn't it? It wasn't by the way, because that was a name that had already been given to her by her birth parents. I'll tell you more about Claire's family later.

No, Brian and Audrey chose the same name as the girl that they had first adopted. Now why would they do that? What chance did that give my sister, hmm? They might as well have called her Mark 2, that's Clare Mark 2. I wonder as a parent now myself, what they would have thought of my sister, given that she had effectively replaced. And what relationship would I have grown to have with the first girl?

So many questions and so few answers.

That's all I know of this time in our very early family years, I was never sure if Claire (that's the second, my Claire) ever knew about it. Guess what? We never ever discussed it in our time together. Plain common all-garden never. You'll see that this steadily became a theme in the Holbrook household, failing utterly to talk about crucial issues or events. I am sure that this was something that Dad and possibly Mum didn't want us to know, they wanted to keep it from us for ever.

If Mum hadn't got so upset that night, perhaps I would never even have found this out.

I wonder what else I don't know? Makes you think doesn't it? It does me.

However, I would have hoped that our relationship with Dad was open and strong enough that he would have chosen to tell us about this as adults, but that didn't happen. Not with Brian Holbrook. Not with our Dad.

I have thought back over the years about Mum on countless occasions. In actual fact, I would not be surprised if I have had thoughts about Mum of some kind every single day, going right back to November 1980 when she left us.

The older I grow, it's a sad fact that the fewer the memories that I have of her. One enduring memory that I do have very clearly is as a boy of about eleven or twelve. I had been playing with a white plastic football in the back garden of 16 Manor Way, and I must have kicked the ball into some rose bushes on the left-hand side border between the two huge oak trees. Tragically for me as a young boy, the ball had burst very quickly. When I went to pick it up out of the bushes, it was already too flat to play with. Not good for my burgeoning soccer career with Manchester United. Definitely them.

Mum was wearing a cream woollen jumper that day I can remember, and she must have seen what happened from the patio. I remember that she went upstairs and came down pretty soon afterwards with a second football that she had bought in case something just like this happened. Thanks Mum, look what an impact you had on my professional soccer career at the crucial stage! For the record, Mum had definitely not been drinking that day, nice memory … very special, all of those years later.

I hope that Mum loved Claire and me. I think that she probably did. We had some wonderful, wonderful, wonderful family friends called The Robinsons with whom we had simply the happiest holidays and Christmases over many years. I'll tell you about them shortly, they were and still are an exceptional bunch of people. Their daughters are simply sensational to look at. I know that in their own way, they were all secretly very attracted to me over the years! All of them. I don't think they quite know how lucky they have mainly been as a family, although they too have had challenges of course. Which family doesn't?

The Mum and Dad to this wonderful family are Audrey and Bud. Audrey, along with Anne Wood and Betty Hitchcock were undoubtedly Mum's very closest friends. I think that there was perhaps something very special between the two Audreys, they were certainly great friends. They had all met in an interesting way sometime in the early 1960s. Mum and Dad lived in a flat at the top of Manor Way in Blackheath, Bud and Audrey lived in what Audrey described to me as a modest house in Grove Park, only a few miles away. Dad had come to be their family GP over some years, and Bud was himself a budding Paediatrician. He came to have a very strong reputation professionally, and I can remember Dad and he having many conversations over the years about medical things. They would compare experiences as we walked through woods in Sussex over the Christmas holidays, and in this way I would come to be comfortable with so many medical terms and what they meant, just from overhearing their conversations. Most of our family friends were from medical backgrounds too. Manor Way should have been renamed "The Road of Doctors" or something like that, not to forget the excellent Surgeons Red O'Flynn and David Jenkins too of course.

Charming, kind and witty men both of them.

No confidences were ever broken in the medical discussions, individuals' names were not mentioned at all, it was just two medical men talking "shop" I guess.

Intelligent and skilled "shop", but "shop" nonetheless.

Dad used to receive the BMJ Journal from the British Medical Association, each month I think. I remember picking up the pale blue and white magazine from the indestructible brown doormat in 16 Manor Way and taking it into Dad, over many years. Dad was particularly good about keeping up with the latest medical research and reports it was a credit to him.

He too was a good and honest medical man with a justifiably strong reputation. As he grew older, the inevitability that he would fall behind with current medical news really concerned him. Dad was a conscientious and dedicated family GP.

Good on you for that bit Dad. Your patients and colleagues respected you greatly, as I did. Perhaps Claire too, at times. Less so later, both of us.

To get back on track re our relationship with Mum, Audrey told me twice that Mum was very happy indeed in the early years when she had us, her children. I don't know if Audrey Rob knew about Mum's first baby girl. My understanding as I grew up as a kid was that Mum had been unable to have children through having "blocked fallopian tubes". I wonder if that is actually medically correct? I could look it up right now, as I am writing this, but I think I'll leave it, it's too deeply ingrained into my past now. I wonder if lots of things that I think I have filed away correctly in my mind about our family are correct. I suspect not.

Anyway, those three words are very closely associated in my mind over a long sustained period of time, "blocked fallopian tubes".

I think that Mum and Audrey, the two Audreys, spent a good amount of time together in the 60s with their children who were growing up. Grove Park and Manor Way are only fifteen minutes drive away, probably less in those days when there would have been way much less traffic on the roads. I remember Dad telling me once that at that time it was quite normal for people who had cars not to wear seat belts, this seems so very strange to us now doesn't it? Anyway, the two Mums with young children would get together in either one of their flats, one in a very elegant Edwardian building, the other situated very handily above a Chemist's shop. GP and Paediatrician were hard at their respective jobs, and so a strong relationship began to develop, and the "Robs" and the "Hollybrooks" became very fine friends. I think. Dad had even been present at the delivery of some of Audrey's children at their home.

16 Manor Way

When the Robs moved away from London as Bud, sorry that should be "Dr Robinson", took up a new post at Chichester in West Sussex, so the relationship stayed in place strongly, and we would visit them at their house in Barnham in Sussex on so many happy occasions. Oakhurst No.146 Main Road. When I was last down there, I found a moment to secretly kiss the brick wall on the side of the house, that's how much my times there meant to me, and mean to me still. Fabulous and happy days for us. If you don't know Barnham, it's where the train from London's Victoria station splits, one section travelling onto Chichester, the other onto exotic Bognor Regis, ("Bognor of the King", from the third declension masculine Latin noun "Rex, Regis", but then again you knew that already of course.)

Possibly the very happiest moments of my childhood were spent in the company of this exceptional family down in Sussex, which has made me wonder on several occasions quite what our own family life was truly like. Many Christmases were spent with them in fact Christmas was not that without being with the Robinsons over the 25th and 26th December.

Audrey told me earlier this year that we had had a "tough" life as kids, which of course would have been very hard for people looking in on our privileged life to really understand. That was the word that she had used, and I think she had reason to select that particular adjective.

I wonder what you meant by that Audrey, I wonder what you can remember, what did you see as an adult that I couldn't as a young adopted child?

What was missing, what should have been there but wasn't?

Where the normality?

Where the family?

Where Clare 1? Where is Clare 1 now?

And did Mum love us like I love my children?

So Mum is so sadly a fading memory to me. We have some photographs of her over the years of course but she didn't like her picture being taken, and I mean really didn't like it! I suspect that she knew only too well the effect that alcohol was having on her looks and didn't want to see it in photos. Perhaps she had known this since her late teens. You had a lovely kind smile Mum and your laugh was just great.

I do remember that she liked animals very much. Mum and Dad had a dog called Cindy that we grew up with. She was a lovely yellow Labrador that was always great to play with, a very loyal and kind dog. She was always known as Mum's dog, and when Dad took Cindy to the vet's at Folkestone in Kent one day after she had clearly been very ill, (the dog not the vet!), I remember walking through the dog daisies in the field opposite Ivy Cottage with Mum. I think Claire was there with us too, waiting expectantly to see how Dad had got on. His car could be been twisting through the lane coming up the hill, passing through the tunnel of trees that hid the route up to our idyllic black and white tudor "Ivy Cottage"in Kent. As he walked briskly up the field to meet us with clear purpose, now without Cindy, we knew that it was sad news and Mum burst into tears, and she stayed that way for much of that hot summer's afternoon.

Funny isn't it how your childhood memories of summer are always of long hot days, while those of winter are of cold and dark ones? That bright summer day was also a dark one for Mum. Cindy had been very special to her. If animals could talk, I wonder what she could have told me about the early years of our family, about Claire one and two, about the drinking, about our Mum and Dad and about their marriage ….?

Woof, woof woof. Tell me what you know Cindy, please. Woof, woof, woof. Things you heard, things you saw, the things that I didn't see or hear or know. Woof, woof, woof.

When Bud and Dad talked about medical things, Mum was kind of on the edge of the conversation. She didn't really seem to want to take part, to listen to any detail, or to contribute at all in fact. Perhaps Dad was right that going into Nursing had only been a way out from Mum of an intolerable family situation in 1950s Stockton-on-Tees. I will never know, I need to start looking forward in my life, the past has already stolen so much from me and particularly from Claire. It seemed that Mum was trying to flee something.

I miss you Mum, each and every day.

If I could start over again with someone that I had met in my past, it would be with you Audrey Moss. We would drink the very best chilled fruit juice on a bright, long summer's day, and holding hands, you would fill in the missing pieces for me from so many years, you would patiently answer all my impatient questions, and I would comfort you, and hug you, and I would feel your pain through my own, and we would come to know each other, like I don't think we have done yet.

What did I mean to you Mum, really? And Claire? What did we mean to you, and did we make your life happier than if we had never met you? Did you love us? Were we important to you? I just don't know looking back. Whatever was going on in your head, or your heart, it took you away from us on the night of 14th November 1980.

Audrey Holbrook, Audrey Hepburn.

Thanks for the second football Mum.

If you want to understand my relationship with Dad, then here's what you do. It really couldn't be more easy. You think of a great father and son relationship that you have witnessed, actually think of possibly more than one. Then think of the father/son relationship that you would hold up to others as an example of a particularly good one, just think of the very best one you can. I hope that this may come from your own family or your circle of friends possibly. Then think further still about a relationship between a father and his son that you would think of as quite exceptional, and try to think too quite why it's like that. Well, for twenty years, from 1961 onwards, I can tell you that the relationship between Brian and Nick was on one whole level above that one that you just thought of. Our relationship was very, very special indeed.

I suppose that looking back on it, Dad and I were mates. We were undoubtedly fishing mates, absolutely no doubts about that! From the age of four, Dad took me fishing. That was probably the very greatest gift that he gave me, I am hoping to go tomorrow afternoon, if the weather's good, that's how integral a part of my life going fishing is. As the fridge magnet downstairs says, (for some reason it's currently actually on the front of the microwave),

"If they don't have fishing in Heaven, I'm not going".

We also played a lot of golf together over the years, but the place where Brian and Nick were most close, was by the bank of an English Lake. That was a wonderful place for us, and for that I know that I am so very lucky. Forgive me while I write this, this will mean nothing to you unless you happen to be a fly fisherman/woman, but I have wanted to put this down in writing for a long time now .... Dad will know what friendship between us lies behind these next words.

"Dad, can you hear me? It's Nick calling you.

Peters Bay, hot summer evening at Bough Beech, weight forward 7 line, 6 lb point, with a large Invicta on. Fish right up in the waves taking sedges, the second rod already set up on the bank with a Baby Doll, for the last knockings, need to back at the hut by 10.30 ... bowl of cereal when we got home at 11.15 at night, after gutting the fish.

Tight Lines Dad, love you."

16 Manor Way

Nick and Brian were very close. That is not something that can ever be guaranteed between two members of a family, perhaps even less so when the child is adopted. However, it is hard in the real world to imagine a relationship with Dad that could have been significantly stronger. He will always be Dad to me, and even if I was to trace my natural father at some point, nothing would ever budge Dad one inch from his position in my heart, ever. We had so many great fly fishing trips together down at Bough Beech reservoir in Kent in particular in the late seventies. Dad taught me how to cast, and how to tie flies and where to find the fish in a huge reservoir of hundreds of acres. I got better than him at catching Rainbow trout on a large still water, but put us together on a river and Dad was ten times better than me. Okay, eight times better, but you get my point. We were good together, really.

We had I guess an open and loving relationship, like how it should be. I never questioned him nor him me. There was complete trust and acceptance and fondness and humour and laughter and guidance and advice when needed and support and encouragement and sheer being there for me. For twenty years, Brian Holbrook was just the best Dad. Isn't that right Dad?

I always, always think of you Dad on September 22nd, and I always looked for humorous birthday cards which I knew you appreciated. Our relationship was just great wasn't it, just great, the absolute best? Completely, like only you and I can ever know.

Miss you so much, as I know others do. The Dad who was nice, the Dad that I loved without question, that's the one that I miss.

Dad had come from a family that grew up in Grapenhall in Warrington, "up North" as we soft southerners say so stereotypically. His Dad was Leonard Holbrook and his Mum, our Granny, was called Myriam. I never met his Dad as he had died before Claire and I came along. There is I think a little mystery around his Dad's death, something to do with a medical condition that should have been picked up better and earlier than it was.

I sensed from fragments of conversation with Dad over the years, rightly or wrongly, that Dad himself felt bad about this as he was close to graduating as a medical student at that time. Leonard, who would have been my grandfather, died when Dad was twenty five and Dad did indeed pass his Medical exams successfully at that early age shortly after his father passed away. I think he was quite fond of his father, and he certainly got his good looks from him. His relationship with his mother was slightly more formal but pretty good I think. If ever the Duke of Edinburgh needed a stand-in at short notice, Dad was your man – "Dad, Philip, say hello, Philip, Dad!"

Dad had a sister, Betty, a couple of years older than him. They looked very similar, same nose and recognisable smile. I've seen Dad in Betty's eyes whenever I have looked into them. I have always thought of her as my Aunt of course and she married a delightful man called Dick. Dick was such a character, he was a vet, sadly he died recently now, and one of the very funniest men you could ever meet, with a lovely dry and ironic sense of humour. He was asked to take part in some programmes on BBC Radio Sheffield some years ago in the 70s/80s and was billed as the "Siegried Farnon" of South Yorkshire, if you remember the books of "It shouldn't happen to a Vet" from those days. Christopher Timothy played the part of James Herriot in the film that they made you may remember.

Dick's best joke was to reply to the question "Doesn't it hurt when you castrate a bull?" with the words "No, not if you don't get your fingers caught between the two bricks!" Not very pleasant I know, but funny when gangly Dick told it to you. Dick Walker, vet of Sheffield, God Bless you, you made our Mum laugh a lot I can definitely remember.

Thanks for making her happy.

So what else should I tell you about Dad? Well, I think you will know by now just how much Dad meant to me. Like Mum, I think about him every living day. I have dreams that he appears in too, so it happens at night as well. I can't tell you how close we were. That was in the first half of the game.

So now I need to tell that he screwed up.

The best way to describe this to you is to ask you first to imagine someone giving you the most wonderful present that they could ever give you. Imagine them handing across something that you had no idea about, something really exciting and of the highest quality possible. Something that you were just plain lucky to receive, something that not everyone gets. Perhaps something that was so very nice that you never really had any expectation that you would actually see or get this. It's a gift that you will remember for ever, that you will talk to other people about or maybe even write about like I'm trying to do here in these pages.

It was actually something that became a cornerstone in your life, no it was more than that, it was your actual foundations. A brilliant just brilliant gift,

"Thank you, it's just what I always wanted", isn't that what we say?

You get the picture.

So now picture this. Some years later, that same person who had given you that gift, (remember that precious present above?), comes back and plain wrenches it out of your hand. That's what Dad did to me. And he did it to Claire. And he did this when we were down and confused and in need of love from our one remaining parent.

I don't think I'll ever understand why the man that I have been describing to you above, my fishing mate did that to us. Nice one Brian. You became a stranger to us - overnight.

What do I mean? Well, let me explain. Mum died in November 1980, as you know by now. For the days, weeks and months immediately afterwards, the three of us, Claire, Dad and I pulled together in some way. Survival. You either go the same way as Mum or you struggle through as best you can, in the hope of days brighter. And that's what we did, we coped, struggled, got on with things, kept busy, made the most of it, did the shopping, kept your head down and got through the day, built a routine and got on with it. Brave Face and all that.

Taking it one day at a time, it'll get better. Christmas 1980 wasn't great mind you, but there you go. We'll be fine. Oh yes, and then there's New Year's Eve coming round fast, perhaps we stayed in that year, I don't recall, it's all a bit of a blur. I don't suppose that my birthday on January 5th 1981, just two months after Mum had died, was much cop either, but "onwards & upwards" as they say.

Friends were fine of course. I remember, vividly, sitting in our "playroom" as we called it, probably only days after Mum had died, with Betty Hitchcock staying with us, watching "Not the Nine O'Clock News" on the television. Dad liked it, he laughed at most of it in fact, and then the terrible dark cloud that had been lifted from you for a few brief and hilarious moments, returned to cover you with its dreadful darkness. Thanks Rowan Atkinson, and team. You brightened the Holbrook household for a few funny moments that night, and how we needed it.

I was in the second year of University at that time, and like I said, we just got on with it. I got my degree which was good but my time at University was just disastrous, so wasted. It all seems a long time ago, in fact it's nearly twenty five years ago since all of this happened. Claire was at Art College in South London, and Dad went back to 121 Trafalgar Road as the good Greenwich GP that he was, and always would be. Shame he didn't apply his professionalism to our family situation though, or his judgement.

I remember that I did most of the family food shopping, at Waitrose in Bromley I remember very clearly. Good middle-class family us you see, Sainsbury's sometimes, mainly in the winter when it was dark and you couldn't been seen going in and out! - (only joking Mr S, nice stores really). We pulled through, we didn't go through any counselling of any kind, unless you count life's monotony as a source of counselling, and from time to time we talked. Dad and I in particular. Claire and Dad on one or two occasions, perhaps Claire and I too and that particularly should have happened so much more. Remember, the three of us came from different sources, three people thrown together by circumstance, impacted on now so enormously by the decision and act of an unhappy young girl from Stockton-On-Tees, who had taken her own life in that same house, upstairs in the spare room one night. I think some tragedy from her own family as a young girl had pursued her, but we didn't know, and I don't suppose that I can ever know now.

I guess the grey carpet in the room where she died has long gone now. The under-felt too. But never the pain.

So, that was how we were. More significantly, things had already started to go wrong at this point. Yes, Mum's death was a thing that had gone wrong of course, but I'm talking about how we reacted and coped and survived. Things were off-track within weeks, and a little imagination might just have addressed that … Dad.

All three of us should have had some professional counselling. What are the words in Charlotte Church's song "I Need Professional Help"? Well, that was us, we all needed it. Dad needed it to begin to come to terms with the death of his wife in his fifties, Dad to come to terms with the fact that she had killed herself and Claire and I to make some sense of this at the age of eighteen and nineteen, and cope as best we could with the help of experienced professionals.

But, guess what? It never happened. You're probably beginning to get the picture by now, crucial conversations that should have happened, stayed locked down. Rather surprising isn't it, when you consider that Dad was a Doctor. That we lived in a Doctors'

Road, surrounded by Medical professionals, and that anyone of them was capable of picking up the phone or writing a letter to the relevant people to get things moving. But, in 16 Manor Way, this never happened.

"Doctors to the right of me, and Doctors to the left, but here I am stuck in the middle in need of counselling ..."

True, we didn't have e-mail widely available in those days like we do now, we couldn't just send off a text message from our mobile phone like we do so often these days, but it's not much of an excuse is it now ? No, the reason that we didn't get help was Dad. It either never occurred to him, or there was something that he wanted to hide.

Remember the present that I asked you to think about earlier? Well, keep it in your mind.
I still had it in my possession at this point. Just.

I was working in Spain, teaching English, in a very tough Boys remedial school in late 1982 and into 1983. It was not something that I particularly wanted to do, but I had applied for Teacher Training in 1983-1984, got my place confirmed at Sheffield University, and so wanted to use my year beforehand well to do something good and worthwhile. It's what we all call the Gap Year now isn't it? Not quite so common then perhaps, but the same thing.

Life in the Colegio San Jose was not great, it was a tough school, a boarding school, the boys were not allowed out of the buildings except at weekends, and to make things a little worse my room was in the refectory. Completely white and antiseptic, it was fine I suppose looking back on it, clean, but rather cold and very basic. Whiter than Persil it was. I wasn't really hugely happy there. The Central Bureau for Educational Visits and Exchanges (CBEVE strangely enough) had not been entirely straight with me about the type of school that they had arranged for me. Could have been a lot better, technically it could have been worse, but it was not great. Still, "C'est la vie" as they say in the country to the top and right of Espana ("asi es la vida"in Spanish of course).

I came home earlier than planned, by a month or so. I was slimmer, lightly tanned, I had done lots of running there, my Spanish was even better (it was good already in a very proper and correctly-structured kind of way), and I had spent time in another country, which was all good. I came back by train, up to Madrid, across and up through the surprisingly lush green countryside of Northern Spain that did a pretty good impression of parts of Switzerland, over to the French border, up to Paris (seriously fast train service that one), and up still further to the French coast to catch the ferry back.

I suffer from motion sickness, I do hate being on a boat, and so I travelled from Dieppe to Newhaven in the freezing February air, sitting outside for almost all of the four and three quarter hour's crossing. Even worse, there was a gale blowing, so I was both cold and nauseous and wet for nearly all of that time. Winning combination huh? But go indoors and you smell the cooked food and diesel fumes and want to be sick, so stay outdoors where you freeze but aren't actually sick. Nice choice eh?!

"You want to make a note of my e-mail address? Sure it's:

"Nicholasholbrook@vomitonthetopdeck.com:

It's those bloody diced carrots, that's what does it you know!!

If you catch the boat from Calais to Dover, at least you can see land all the time, France or Kent. Fellow sufferers of travel sickness will know that it's hugely helpful to be able to see a horizon on which to be able to focus, that reduces the chance of you being sick greatly, possibly by as much as seventy or eighty percent in my not inconsiderable experience. Reminds me of that classic joke of the two guys standing on the deck of the boat, where one is obviously being very ill vomiting away. Man no. 1 says to the other

"What's the matter, can't you reach?"

and the other guy replies, with some difficulty

"Reach? What you talking about, I'm throwing it as far out as I can!"

Funny huh?

So, Newhaven in February 1983, despite the cold and the fog and the wind out at sea, was fine for me. I was back in England. I don't remember the kind of clothes that I had in those days, nor the suitcase or holdall that I must have brought back with me, nor anything about the train journey back to London, but I must have made it back somehow, all quite legally I am sure, despite having very little money.

"Hasta la proxima vez Espana", see you soon.

I was home at 16 Manor Way. Looking back on it, I don't remember Dad being pleased to see me back. Not at all. Not in the slightest.

I don't recall the Father/Son hug after several months apart like my son Jack and I would certainly give each other.

I think I would remember if he had taken great interest in my trip aboard, on where I had been, where I had been staying, who I had met etc…. but I don't think you did that Dad. Not at all. Not in the slightest.

Claire and I would have caught up too somewhere. I think she was going out with a nice guy called Robin around that time, lived over in Lock Chase. Claire seemed very fond of him I remember. Claire was into the cord jeans and "heavy on the mascara" look in those early 1980s days. Boy George, HairCut 100, Tiswas time, if that means anything to you.

16 Manor Way

I think a change had happened in Dad. What am I saying "I think"? I don't believe that I consciously registered this at the time, why would I? Why was our Dad ever going to change? After all, he's our Dad, a constant in our lives. He's always going to be there for us, isn't he? Isn't he? Isn't he? Dad, Dad, our Dad. Especially since Mum has gone, right?

But deep down, I must have noticed, how else could I be remembering this so very clearly over twenty five years later? He was colder. He was less warm. He was less there for us, he was moving to another place. What was happening in fact was that he was moving to another person, Diana. And he was going away from us, for ever as it was to turn out.

I never really considered around that time if Dad would re-marry. I was a rather confused and wounded twenty-two year old at this point, - beard, gold John Lennon round student sunglasses, button-down collar shirts and pencil tie if I really had to wear one at all. Wrestling with adoption and Mum's suicide, Claire and I. Not feeling sorry for ourselves, really, but definitely needing and wanting to make some sense of our existence.

Seems reasonable to me, doesn't it to you?

I don't think that my brain had ever entertained the idea of Dad going out with anyone else, and yet while I was away in Spain things had been going on. It all makes sense now, looking back on that time when Dad seemed lukewarm about me coming back early from Spain. Hum.

Then, before you knew it, Dad was in the bathroom one evening getting ready for something, having a shave that Spring evening, and I commented something like "Having a shave in the evening Dad, that's not like you ?" He replied that he was going out with someone for the evening, but not in Dad's voice. He might just as well have added … "if that's all right with you Nick?" The water in the sink might have been warm, but not our Dad. His tone was that cold.

A little challenging too. He was changing in some way, and for the worse.

Change, followed by the sudden whirlwind that I had not heard coming. We were in the quiet before the storm I think, but we were absolutely unaware of any of this at the time.

Some weeks later, the four of us went to London to eat a meal out in a restaurant called "The Gay Hussar" near Leicester Square, and then weeks after that they were getting married in Woolwich Town Hall. Not the Hussar, he stayed in London with all of his gay friends, but our Dad and this complete, total, new, and unwelcome stranger. No introduction, no segue way as they say in the US, no selling things to Claire and I, no conversations between the three of us about

"We all need to move on and I want you to know that I've met someone that I like"

speech, no lead-up to it, no subtlety, no fucking imagination at all you bastard.
Crap Dad, utter cold and crap Dad.

0-60 in one second, "…oh and by the way she's moving in next month, she'll be sleeping with me in your Mother's bed, and oh yes I'm giving her your mother's watch, she's going to be wearing it from now on, and right in front of you.

Don't talk about Mum, don't refer to her, no conversations about our family or family holidays, no pictures around the house of Mum or us as a family at all, if you do talk about Mum I'll cut you off in mid-sentence, no references to good times that we had, we probably didn't actually, oh and what would you like for Christmas, Diana and I were thinking of getting you some vouchers. Would WH Smiths be okay? Hmm?

Everything okay is it kids, you seem quiet?"

Do you know where the greatest pain was? It wasn't that there were no pictures in the house of Mum, nor that we couldn't talk about her, nor that we had to listen to the shit that "Diana has had a hard life too kids you know" which he actually said to me once. If I was more self-confident, I should have hit my father at that point, asked him as he lay on the ground beneath me what the hell he thought Claire and I have gone through with adoption, Mum's drinking for as long as we can remember, and our Mum putting a plastic bag over her own head one night and suffocating herself, and then walked away from him. Fucking shit Father, in fact not a father at all.

For ever.

I wish that I had done that. But I couldn't. You see I was dependent on him. It was a moment in a person's life where you are wrenched by some great hand above and shown a crossroads, and told to choose, and choose now!

How I wish I had found the confidence to stick two fingers up and go.

A SHORT PLAY NOW FOLLOWS – it has only one act and one very short scene.

Act1, scene 1 – enter Dad, stage left.

Dad's line:

"About your gift. Now I'm grabbing it back from you. There, you don't have it any more."

Exit Dad.

END OF PLAY. ALL GO HOME.

I am reading an excellent book at the moment called "Crucial Conversations" about things that simply must be said, and how best to say them. This was the best example of a crucial conversation from my own life that I can give to you …. But it was never said, and it so should have been. I'm referring to the frank and hard conversation between Nick and his Dad.

The thing that hurt me most was that he was discarding all that we had as a family. The cornerstone, the foundations, our bedrock, the source of our sanity and stability. He was throwing it away, and he was doing it in an instant, apparently without a thought for the consequences or for others. He was supposed to be looking after us, and us after him too, but this stranger had no awareness whatsoever of his impact. In short, he had come back and wrenched the present that he had given us, out of our hands, so very painfully.

You betrayed us Brian Holbrook. Fuck you for what you did to us.

I can live you with you doing that to me. I can't live with you doing that to Claire, or to the memory of the lovely lady that was our Mum, no matter how much there may have been about her that I never knew.

Not Mum, Dad.

Fuck you.

Chapter 3 – What exactly is "normal"?

Why did no-one do anything?

You know what I mean by the word normal don't you? Sure you do. Normal is what happens most of the time, right? Normal. It's what you do time after time isn't it? You know what I'm saying, loads of normal things. It's the regular patterns that you adopt, it's how you spend most of your life, it's what you do repeatedly. Stuff, normal everyday stuff.

So, on this basis, most of the time, I guess that our family too did normal things. Normal things just like everybody else.

My father was a GP and he went to work. Pretty normal then. My mother was a "housewife", which has become a slightly uncomfortable word for us to use nowadays hasn't it? But it was fine to use then in the 60s & 70s. It was normal for many women to be a housewife and a Mum, at least in the area where we lived in Blackheath in South London. Mum had been a nurse for some years and I guess that Dad earned enough money for her not to need to work. Maybe she didn't want to work, I don't know. You see, there are lots of things about my family that I'm not really sure about. More and more things become apparent as I have my own family and look back on those times. We did some normal things yes, but there were also things in our lives that were anything but normal. So I guess we might all conclude from this then that "normal" is a relative term. We had our normality at no. 16 but it was significantly different to what was normal for other folks in Manor Way. We weren't normal at No. 16.

Now, we lived a comfortable life, a very comfortable life in fact. In that respect, let it be said that we were hugely fortunate. We had a lovely house, 16 Manor Way, in Blackheath, London SE3 9EF, also originally named "Eskdale" though we never thought of it with that name. Manor Way was what you might call quite a posh road on what was known locally as the Cator Estate. It was a private estate, built on the site of a large house and grounds originally, and in the 1960s it still had unmade roads. I can remember Dad driving very slowly up the road to our house, past all of the other medical families' homes, going over large stones and broken brick which made up most of the road surface then. In the winter, the puddles were like something out of a comic book. You know the type where the cartoon character, in something like medieval "Tom and Jerry", throws his cloak over a modest puddle to allow the Lady cat to walk across to prevent her getting wet, and when she steps onto his cloak, smiling and flirting with the chivalrous Tom ever so slightly, she unexpectedly sinks down into this apparently small puddle to an impossible depth! You know the cartoon don't you?

Well, that's how our road was, all the way along, and right outside our house in the 60s & 70s.

You had to drive very slowly for several hundred yards, or it could have done some serious damage underneath to your car. I guess it was tarmac-ed over in the late 1970s, but that rough, broken road surface really made the traffic move slowly. You just had no choice!

Nice suburb, lovely family house, very poor road surface.

Dad was a GP in what was then called a Group Practice near Greenwich. As the name suggests, he was one of several GPs who had their own surgery in one single facility. I think they all shared a receptionist or maybe two or perhaps three, and a general waiting area for their sickly patients. Each family doctor had their own private consulting room within the one building.

As a kid, I always liked the idea of my wonderful Dad, my hero then, coming out of his room around 11 am, to have a mid-morning cup of coffee with his colleagues and discussing interesting cases with his fellow GPs. I don't know if he ever did do that but it's a rather warming and comforting idea don't you think? I am sure you did Dad, lots of times. "Dr 'olebrook" as you were affectionately known in Greenwich, London SE10.

Their practice was on Shooters Hill Road in Blackheath, on the side of what is known as the "Sun in Sands" roundabout. It's named after a pub on the edge of the same roundabout. I used to hear Chris Tarrant on Capital Radio talking with Russ someone, his "eye is the sky", and Russ would give Chris reports back about how traffic was moving slowly on its way up to London, and was sometimes "backed up all the way to the Sun in Sands roundabout." Well Russ, you were flying your little plane over the surgery where my Dad had his practice mate, and where he worked for many years as a GP. Chocks away, Russ!

So, normal, it was apparently all very normal.

Claire, my sister, was at secondary school locally in Blackheath. We both went to a private primary school called Riverston, that it was rumoured turned out to be quite a money-maker for Mr and Mrs Lewis the Headmaster of the school and his wife. It was a very friendly school from what I can recall, and I have nothing but deeply fond memories of it. My great fishing chum Guy Beech went there too. It would have been a private house to begin with. I remember the large staircases and high-ceilings in all of the established classrooms. It was always undergoing some kind of development when we were pupils there, and it gradually began to take over the property next door, which then became the new Riverston Junior School. There was a very large playing-field behind the school, which you couldn't see as you drove past, and I am certain that that particular space would be worth a great deal of money now on its own, millions of quid probably.

I believe that Claire and I had some very happy years there, I certainly did. The thing that I most remember about it was the Christmas card postal system that they had in the school. Probably nothing amazing when you stop and think about it now, but for me as an eight or nine year-old, it was just great to be able to post a Christmas card to someone else one morning in the school's little red-post boxes that they had created all over the site, and see it arrive successfully the following day. And here's the best bit, no stamp was needed! It didn't cost a penny, what a great service. My kind of Post Office!

When I started there at about the age of seven, Mum took me there a full day early! What are you like Mum?! What were you thinking Mum? Honestly, get yourself a Filofax or a Blackberry or something … I can still remember this so clearly thirty seven years later, Mrs Lewis the Headmistress bending down and saying nice things to me about being a day early and "don't worry about it darling because you can come back tomorrow and that's when all of the other boys and girls will be starting too, so that'll all be quite fine Nicholas really…" Could have happened to anyone, getting the wrong day for the start of term Mum for their child, don't worry about it.

I wonder if that's all there was to it? Mum? No other reason?

Dad picked us up from Riverston in his new car one day. Brand new, from Penfold's of Lewisham just down the road. Do you know what it was? Well I'll tell you. This would have been around 1970 I guess, our Dad arrived in a White Automatic Vauxhall Ventora, now have you ever heard of that? White with a black vinyl roof to be precise, and with an automatic gearbox I seem to remember. Actually, he seemed very unsure about the Ventora from day one. I don't remember how long he had it but he said that it rusted away very quickly. It must have done exactly that bloody fast because I can only remember him collecting us in it on that one day! Perhaps he didn't have it very long at all, he had quite a few cars did Dad, as I shall get round to telling you later.

So after Riverston, Claire went to Blackheath High School, a private senior school for girls. This was located in Blackheath, on the edge of the heath itself, and was a pretty good school with a good reputation. It was a private, fee-paying school that went all the way up to A level. I seem to remember for some reason that it was very good on Drama and the Sciences in particular. It was still unusual then for girls to do well at the sciences but

Blackheath High did a good job on that front. I think it produced quite a lot of girl Doctors and Engineers.

Anyway, I think that Claire was happy there, not that she was ever going to go down either of those career paths. God had given her real artistic skills you see, which she would use in her life all too infrequently. You were really good Claire, really you were. I have some of your drawings in our home now. Me and art? I couldn't draw a salary me.

The girls wore a dark blue uniform with a rich yellow and blue woollen scarf and the ranks of "BHS girls" could all be seen streaming down into Blackheath Village at going-home time. I don't remember all of the detail, but Mum seemed to get on very well with the Headmistress there. I'm afraid I don't even remember her name, (not Mum's, she was called Mum). Things came about that in a note to Mum one day, the Headmistress made a comment for some reason about "your super son". That was me, yes really. I'd have been about twelve at the time, and was already exceptionally handsome, of course. No really. Dad made a comment back to me about not letting it go to my head, but I remembered that very clearly. Even now.

I like compliments you see, and I like people to like me. Matters to me a great deal. I like people to be nice to me and to pat me on the back. I needed it then. I need it now. I don't like unpleasant people.

After leaving Riverston in 1970, I went to a different school on the other side of London, Dulwich College Preparatory School. Very good school was DCPS, very good indeed although I had no true awareness of this at the time. It was and still is an excellent boys' "prep school" as we call it and DCPS certainly lived up to that name! The amount of prep that we were asked to do each night was unreal, and into the weekends too. Oh yes, and Saturday morning school too, every weekend up until Saturday lunchtime. Five and a half days' school each week, trying getting that past our children these days! They'd all go on the internet to talk to their mates and arrange to go on a mass strike for that whole week, and they'd text each other on how unfair it was that parents make them go to school on the weekend too. More than likely one of them would take the highest possible quality of legal advice or appeal to the European Commission on Human Rights!

You think I'm kidding?

Still, for me you have to understand this was entirely normal. My fishing chum Guy went there too. We used to drive past Dulwich College on the way to the Prep each day, it's a separate school from where I went despite the similar names. Huge duck pond on the corner of the road I remember although it's probably a lot smaller than this little eleven year-old thought it was.

I was never aware that there was any connection between the two schools other than that they were both very near to each other in Dulwich, and that boys from the "Prep" would often go onto the College. If they passed the rigorous Entrance Exam that is.

We used to get to Dulwich from Blackheath about fourteen miles away, not by anything as common as public transport you understand, but by private and probably very expensive taxi. Each day, there and back, five or six times a week. "Eeh, luxury!" The cab company was run by Mr Simmonds, a very friendly man who would have been in his sixties then I would say. "Dopey" Simmonds as we unkindly called him, (sorry we were kids), had a silver Zephyr, remember those? Like the one they had in "The Sweeney" with Dennis Waterman and John Thaw. It was silver, with black vinyl interior (don't think it was leather) and a cool column gear-change. I remember that it also had a bench seat running right across the front. We never wore seat belts in those days and yet we'd go the twenty five miles or more each way six days a week from Blackheath to Dulwich and back to Blackheath, fortunately without incident over the five years. My mate Guy Beech, David and Richard O'Flynn and another nice lad Richard Pell, son of yet another Blackheath GP. Less traffic on the roads then than now I guess but we never had any kind of car accident.

16 Manor Way

One of Mr Simmonds' younger drivers Steve had a Green Ford Cortina four door saloon, the 1600 E I think, and let me tell you that he was not a slow driver!! Even at that age, I can remember not particularly liking it if it was Steve that picked us up from school at the end of the day. Bit rapid was Steve. Still, cool car Steve. Mark II in metallic green,

"Nice wheels mate".

Mr S started an unusual habit about three years into driving us to school each day. One Saturday morning, he stopped at the gent's toilets near Herne Hill to go and answer the call of nature, as you do, to go and see a man about a dog, siphon the python, drain the lizard, you know the sort of thing right? As he got back into the car on one particular morning, he put his hands into his pockets of his rather worn out sheepskin coat (well you had to have one of those if you drove a Zephyr didn't you?), and pulled out a loose handful of Foxes Glacier Mints. He then very kindly offered them to all of us boys in the car. You may know the sweet that I mean here, the confusing Fox's transparent sweet that has a polar bear on the wrapper!

"Miss Jones, get me the head of Marketing into my office Monday 9 am!!"

We always joked, being puerile schoolboys, how lucky it was there were always mints in the gents' toilets when Mr Simmonds went in there in the morning. Once I said insensitively "Thankyou Mr Simmonds" as he got back in the car but before the hand had even gone into the trademark sheepskin, and I got a dirty look from him. Very. I didn't like that, I felt very bad about saying it. God Bless you Mr Simmonds for you and your fellas driving us there safely for five years, without our sealtbelts on, eating Foxes Glacier mints, and you with your bladder now comfortably empty. I wonder where that Zephyr is now?

"Oi Dennis, you seen me motor mate?"

Once at school, other challenges were waiting for us. Bit like Harry Potter going to Hogwarts it was. Maths lessons for starters… I have to tell you that I was simply terrified of Miss Herbertson. We're all terrified of some teacher at some point in our lives aren't we, and it was Miss Herbertson that did it for me. She taught maths, which was not the best of beginnings for me, as technically I wasn't very strong at maths.
"Crap" is the word that comes to mind actually. It was the numbers that got me apart from that I was fine. I would remind you that there are three types of people when it comes to maths, those that are good at it and those that aren't.

She had taught there at DCPS for two hundred and thirty seven years before retiring, which is a fine professional achievement don't you agree ? I wonder how many little boys she put the fear of God into during that time? Let's briefly do the maths on this shall we then? You won't mind me using a calculator here…

Twenty in a class each year, x thirty seven, I make that roughly 740. That's 740 young men who bravely went out into the world from DCPS with a deep-seated fear of bespectacled female Maths teachers in Brown tweed suits who use to sit on the wooden lunch tables in the Main Hall making the wood sag and groan audibly under her considerable bulk. I still shudder thinking about it now! I don't imagine the creaking wooden tables forgot it in a hurry either. Perhaps we should rename "The fear of God" and call it "The Fear of Herbie, as we affectionately called her.

So, Miss H for Maths. A lovely and particularly sexy young teacher called Miss Watson was my first form teacher, coincidentally her mother was an excellent school cleaner at Riverston where Claire and I had been before. Mr Gilbey-Mackenzie for French – brown leather jackets, flash yellow BMW coupe, smoker of Russian specialist tobacco, distinctive goaty beard, distinctive and ever so camp – and Mr Finn the New Zealand Geography Teacher. Then a year or so later there was another Maths Teacher Mr Shakeshaft, who helped me to make a spectacular recovery in the post-Herbertson era. Mr

Closebrooks for English – he got nicknamed Mr ClothesBrush, hell we were good – Nelly Smith also for Geography, (seriously brylcreamed black hair), Mr Ashenhurst for history and his distinctive tall wife Mrs Ashenhurst (strangely enough) for Art, which I rather enjoyed. I've still got one of my pots from her pottery sessions actually, Mr Woodcock the Headmaster whose nickname was "Aaaargh, splinters", (I'll let you work that painful one out for yourself) and finally Mr Rowett for Latin.

Now he was cool Mr Rowett, but in a slightly concerning way, as he would take the whole class talking aloud in nothing but Latin throughout. Not a word of English. That was probably a good technique at a senior school level as a discipline for a secondary school teacher of languages, but I'm not so sure for our young age. Now remember that I was eleven at the time, and he would walk into the room exactly like John Cleese, except for a ginger goaty beard and a completely different name too, saying

"Ambulo, Ambulo, Ambulo".

Full marks for the triple repetition in order to enforce the word "ambulo" to the class, but something wasn't quite connecting in little Nicholas' head as it took me two full terms quite literally to realise that "Ambulare" (infinitive) is "to walk". Perhaps it was me! I did make genuinely terrific progress with Latin after that for the record but it was a slow beginning. I chose to take it at A level so you know. Still, Mr Cleese if you ever need a double, here's your man, in a slightly subdued light maybe, with the curtains partially drawn, and black sunglasses on. Oh, different name too, but don't suppose that matters now does it?

"Ambulo, ambulo, ambulo !" I very much hope that he is alive and well, and still walking briskly somewhere in West London. God bless our teachers, and you first of course Miss Herbertson.

One hell of a character was Mr Rowett - Unus hellofus characterus Rowett erat.

Later there was Mr Ferris also for French, Mr "Thunderguts" Maclean for Latin further up the school, who when a pupil had given a wrong answer in class, would look at them with a deeply withering glance, run his hand over his infrequent hair and say with a note of pure Scottish exasperation

"Oh, don't be fantastic boy!"

(that was fantastic in the old sense you understand of coming up with an answer that came from the land of fantasy). I rather liked Mr Maclean, and I think he quite liked me. I was getting damned good at Latin by now. I liked Latin very much as a subject you see, and I also liked it if people liked me too. I do like people to like me. It matters to me, very much.

So not a bad all-round situation really when I come to think of it, going to a very good school. DCPS was down the road from a large Comprehensive next door to the Prep, called Kingsdale.

One day, I must have been about eleven or twelve I guess, we were walking back from the school playing fields at the end of a warm spring day, and the kids from Kingsdale had come out already. I remember distinctly a group of girls from the school, running up to me and one of them said "Where you've been all my life then Darling?" and they continued to come right up to me, and I backed away from them so much so that I fell over a little white fence in someone's garden and the girls just laughed at me and carried on. Not a brave twelve year-old was I, not much street "Cred" there was there really?

"If you can't look after yourself on the streets of Dulwich in South London Nick, what hope New York, eh?" Or even up in York?! Actually, there were some older boys there too in the gang, for the record, but I remember being most scared of the girls. Best move on, eh? (Nowadays I'd pay a lot of good money to have a group of women dressed as school girls come up to me and push me down onto the ground and stand there looking at me, funny how time changes you isn't it ? Oh well, that's time for you....)

16 Manor Way

Kingsdale was a pretty good local comp from what I remember, quite large but a good school for the record. So, this was what my four years were like at one of the very top prep. schools in the country. It was a clearly very privileged environment in which to go to school, no doubt about it. Many of the boys there came from middle-class professional families and backgrounds. Many of our friends' fathers were Doctors or Surgeons or Senior Specialists in some kind of medical area – Josh McColl's Dad was a surgeon and David and Richard's father Red was too. In fact when Red O'Flynn died just before he was going to retire, they published his obituary in the Daily Telegraph, that's how highly-regarded he was.

I remember one day my mother finding a lump on one of her breasts that she was naturally very concerned about (the lump, not the breast). My Dad was also noticeably concerned, and it was to Red O'Flynn that he turned for urgent medical advice that same evening. I can't be sure when this was, probably around 1973, and I remember my father telling me only very briefly what the matter was and that they were going to get a "second opinion" from Red. I guess Mum got the all-clear but I don't remember Dad ever sitting down and talking with Claire and I about it.

Didn't happen. Normal then, you see this was our strain of normality, the Holbrook variant. Crucial conversations that never got to happen.

The more I think about it, I think Dad had a difficulty in being really open about things with us as kids. There were few things that he wouldn't talk about with you if you asked him to, but he certainly didn't face up to the big conversations or issues that needed to be faced up to. At least if he did talk with you about a particular topic, he wouldn't dig into them much beyond the surface, he just didn't go as far as was needed. The discussion was rarely a lengthy one if you know what I mean. And sometimes in this little life, you really do need to stick with something until you're properly done, don't you? Get it properly aired, let it be discussed openly and ideally widely understood too, so that it's put to bed, well and truly. Then at least things might change for the better, and you can move on.

But Dad didn't do that, he was a very non-confrontational man was Brian Holbrook.

There's a lot of that same quality in me too. My wife Sue sees that, and often makes comment on it. I used it to very good effect early in my work as a teacher at secondary school when I was in my twenties. I taught Spanish language and literature to A level standard, and some French too, and I loved the work. A good school can be a very special place, sometimes a very protective community. Very few students were difficult with me, and I was excellent at diffusing a situation that was potentially difficult. I can't think of a single bust-up or major discipline problem in my five years in teaching. So, the non-confrontational approach is good, right? Maybe, however I'm learning quite steadily now in my forties that it may not be as good a quality to have as I've always thought. At times in a person's life, there are bridges to be crossed, questions to be asked, things to be said and even positions to be taken. This didn't happen with our Dad as I would have liked it to looking back, and we're paying for that now. I reckon I pay for it in lots of ways and very often. I need to face up to situations sometimes much earlier, and I don't do that. "Fight or Flight?" Flight is my default definitely.

So you can see that on first glance Claire and I had a very fortunate education at this early stage in our lives. We were sent to very nice private schools in south London in the 1960s and 1970s, with small class sizes, generally good teachers and we had two parents who presumably cared that we did well very at school. My education would have been very similar to my father's who went to Ambleside in the Lake District and to Worksop College. Mum's education? Couldn't tell you, I don't ever recall talking about Mum's schooling. All I do remember is that she had one particular toy that she loved as a kid called "Tommy Brick." I wonder where Tommy is now, eh?

16 Manor Way

Around this time, Dad's Mum passed away, around 1972 I would guess "Granny" as she was fondly known to us. I quite liked her, Claire didn't like here at all, I think that she was scared of her. I wonder what Granny thought of us, I wonder what thoughts went through her head as she picked us up knowing that we were not really her son's children, that we were not really her grandchildren? I think that there was a distance there to be sure. I don't remember great affection, it's not evident in the few photos that we have left. I can just remember Dad going up to Warrington by train from London quite regularly as Granny Holbrook was getting ill and going to see her "up North". He used to catch the train from King's Cross, and I remember Dad telling us one day that he had got angry with the guard on one occasion because he wouldn't let Dad go through the gate and board the train as it was about to leave. Dad wasn't happy about that atall. Imagine that, non-confrontational Dad being angry with a British Rail guard? He was probably just doing his job. The guard, I mean.

What a huge contradiction it is that you remember these little details many years later, and yet can also have such yawningly large gaps of knowledge about your own family and the relationships within it. Perhaps our minds work that way, maybe they cling on desperately to small moments and memories in this way to compensate for the absence of the greater memories. I'm not qualified in psychology in any way at all, but I'm sure that this can not be too far from the truth. I have almost no memories of Mum for instance, and yet the ones that I do have, are burned with a searing heat into my memory so that I can't ever forget them. I'm sure they fight off time you know, and re-burn themselves every now and then into my memory, I'm sure that something like that happens. I remember the clothes that she was wearing on the Saturday that she died, the radio with the Radio 4 programme in the background, and the lunchtime meal of pork that she had cooked on that autumn Saturday. Not the "Last Supper", more "The Last Lunch" actually of roast pork as she listened to "The World at One" on her greasy Roberts radio in the small kitchen that we had in our house. Cream coloured polo-neck jumper, probably a very good quality one too, and beige skirt.

Not the Roberts radio, Mum.

I liked Granny very much, Claire was scared of her. I remember her smile and her warmth, and we've got some nice pictures of me on her lap as a young baby in the first flat that Mum and Dad lived in at the top of Manor Way. They're black and white photographs but they're very good quality. Dad would have taken the pictures I'm sure (you can tell this easily as he's not in many of them!), and he would almost certainly have developed them himself too. He was very good at that was Dad, "a dab hand" was the phrase that he'd have used.

He had customised a small cupboard in the flat at No.96 Manor Way that he had converted into a dark room where he'd develop the photos himself. They're nice photos printed on a high quality paper, but I don't have many of them left now.

The ones that I have, I so treasure. You took good pictures Dad.

I wonder what Granny thought of so many things as Claire and I grew up, her adopted grandchildren? I don't really know for instance what she thought of Mum, her daughter-in-law. Did they get on, were they good friends? I think they probably were as far as I know. I've got no reason at all to think that they didn't get on, and again some of Dad's great 1950s/60s photographs show them walking arm in arm walking along a beach for instance, with Granny in a very stylish tweed suit and hat, and Mum in a wonderful thick white coat which I remember to this day. You looked like a classic Norman Parkinson model Mum, really. Maybe it wasn't Dad who took the photos after all, maybe it was Norman Parkinson who took them all, and I was just never told! Nice thought isn't it?

Good job Norman, you've done that before haven't you?

16 Manor Way

Whoever it was that took them during those years, they certainly did a great job. Great because they are nice photos of elegant people in their own right, but also because we have so little to remind us of Mum and Granny.

Maybe Mum and Granny were particularly close, as Mum's own mother had died when she was young. Or so I had been told, from a young age. Perhaps Audrey Moss/Holbrook and Myriam Holbrook were very close indeed, I'd very much like that to have been the case. Mum had a very large black hole in here life too I'm sure and maybe Dad's Mum helped to fill that in some way. Never will quite know what made the hole. What thoughts passed through their minds I wonder as these two elegant women walked together, with autumnal leaves blowing around them both and tea and toast waiting for them inside.

Nice coat Mum, Norman Parkinson would most definitely have approved.

Audrey Hepburn, Audrey Holbrook. Stars.

Mum learned to drive around this time, and Granny at first leant her a car to learn on. It sounds strange that now doesn't it, as we live in a world when seventeen year-olds often have their first driving lesson on their 17th birthday itself. There was our Mum learning to drive I guess in her thirties, how times change. It was an Austin 1100 that was to be her first carriage, in dark green, manual of course. Another 60s classic. Mum then passed her driving test pretty quickly I think and I can remember her driving us around in the 1100 as very young kids. Granny subsequently sold this car to Mum and Dad. No sorry, I don't know the price, but that would have been Mum's very first car. Dad was almost certainly in a Mercedes around this time, a good car for a South London GP to be driving around in, eh? Liked his Mercs did Dad.

I think that they may have benefited financially quite a lot from Granny towards the end of her life. I reckon that she gave them a very good price on the green 1100. "Haggling not required" within the Holbrook family.

I wonder how Dad got on with his Mum at this point, I wonder how close they were, what they talked about, what they could and could not say to each other. I wonder what Granny thought about Dad's wife, about his choice of wife, the lady who became our Mum, and what she Granny thought about the fact that her son and his wife could not have children of their own. Do you think that Dad and she discussed this? If so, did they talk about this briefly or in some detail? When and where did they talk? I can't tell you, but I think Dad looked up to his Mum, our Grannny, and would have showed her great respect at all times. I think he loved her, but I think he was slightly in fear of her. Perhaps even a little like I was of Miss Herbertson at school.

Dad's Dad was called Leonard Venables Holbrook, what a fine name. Dad looked just like him, upright, slightly thinned hair, warm and compassionate, always with a trusting slight smile on his face. My Dad was a good man, and I think that Leonard probably was too. Sadly, I never knew him, as he had died before I was put together. He died of something like blood poisoning when Dad was training at Medical College, and the news of his father's death had been kept from Dad by a day or so as he was finishing off his medical finals at that time. At least, that was what I was told, by Dad I think. Dad did really well as a medical student and qualified whilst still twenty two, not yet twenty three, which was exceptionally young. He was at St. Bartholomews ("Barts") in London, and I think that he enjoyed himself there very much, as well as working hard. Dad would never tell me the whole story around his father's death and I still don't know to this day exactly what happened. I have this lingering memory in my mind, and not without some justification I think, that Dad was involved in giving his father medical advice at the time to help him, but I don't think that he got it fully right, something like that. I can't tell you any more than that but it was something along these lines. Not all good I think.

16 Manor Way

We didn't really talk about Grandad as he would have been to us, or about Granny's death. Dad didn't really talk through these kind of things with us ever, and yet we were screaming out as bright and inquisitive kids to know about our family and the key figures in it.

Perhaps it was a generation thing. Perhaps it was a Northern thing. Certainly it came to be a Holbrook thing.

What a difference to how I chose to tell Jack and Sophie about my own Dad's death. It was a simply extraordinary and impactful moment earlier this year. I had been to see Dad in the Red Lion Nursing Home in Canterbury that Saturday, and had been with him most of the day.

I left around 10 pm that night, and drove back to Berkshire from Kent, getting home about 11.45 pm. I spoke with Sue briefly who was still up and about, I think we had the ubiquitous cup of tea, and I then I went to have a shower to freshen up before going to bed. I couldn't have been in the shower for more than twenty or thirty seconds, when Sue came in to the bathroom and told me that the Nursing Home were on the phone and that I needed to talk with them. It was the very lovely black Night Nurse Pauline who I had been speaking to only two hours before in the Nursing home who was on the line, and who told me very quietly and very professionally and so well:

"Nicholas, your Dad passed away".

Wow, what a moment for me ……………………..my hero had died.

The following morning, I went down to Sussex to tell Claire the news. I had done my best to prepare her in the preceding days and I don't think it shocked her, and yet it did just that of course, fully. How could it not? Claire and I walked across to the local Café in the High Street in Steyning in Sussex and somehow found ourselves eating a huge full English breakfast each in this café!

I don't think you're supposed to do that when you've just had bad news are you? You're supposed to be confused and upset and off all food and drink, but we ate well and I remember that we both had extra toast too. Perhaps we'd been letting go of Dad over many, many, many, years. Perhaps his continuous not being there for us when we so needed him to be, had gradually numbed our relationship with him month after month, such as it had once been, to the point that when he died, it was the logical and expected final step in a steadily degrading relationship that had got to a point where it was without any kind of true value or honesty.

That's exactly what happened, and it happened over twenty two years Dad.
How unbelievably sad, when I know what we once had.

Discarded.

Fucking sad isn't it?

Just ten percent more imagination Dad and fifteen percent more backbone on your part in standing up to your jealous second wife, and how very different it might have been.

No, how different it would have been. Maybe that way, when I went down to Sussex to see your daughter to tell her that you had died the night before she would have burst into inconsolable sadness, instead of which Claire said to me

"Has he gone then?"

and I replied

"He has".

Dad, I'd like you to know that we both had extra toast that sad morning, both of us, the day after our Dad had died. We were hungry, and on that day we both needed to eat. We had other needs too Dad, but you stopped being aware of those a long, long time ago, when you became a total stranger to the both of us.

When I got back home from seeing Claire, I spent some time with the family and then made some time to sit down with Jack and Sophie.

I sat them down in their play room as we call it downstairs and said that I had something that I needed to tell them, and it went something like this ....

"Darlings, you know that Grandad Brian has been very ill these past few weeks. We saw him in hospital didn't we, and he wasn't really very strong, do you remember? He couldn't walk or get up, and needed to stay in bed all the time now. He was very weak, and even talking or eating a small meal was rather difficult for him. Then the Doctors said that we was settled enough to go into a Nursing Home, where he would get looked after by the nurses there twenty four hours a day if he needed this. Now, Mummy and Daddy have been to see him a lot recently, and Daddy was down with him all day yesterday do you remember? I left him about ten o'clock at night time, and then drove back home here. I had been talking with him lots and had been holding his hand loads of times during the day and I'd said some very nice and important things to him during the day, and that mattered to me a lot. Well, when I get home last night, the Nurse Pauline who was looking after him during the night called me. She said that his breathing had been very difficult, he wasn't eating or drinking anything at all, he was now asleep all the time. I wasn't able to talk with him at all when I was there, and then during the night when I was driving back he got a little bit worse, just after I had seen him, and then he had really given up on fighting and so he just slipped away ... and he died I'm afraid ..." (I'm crying as I write this).

I then broke down at that point and our wonderful, marvellous, magical children both burst into tears with Sue and I there to hold them and cuddle them. They were very, very, very sad that you had died Grandad. They were very fond of you, and I wanted you to know that.

And I had loved you too more than was possible. Any you had stopped loving me.

Sophie, your nine year-old granddaughter (then) went out and bought a new dress and cardigan so that she could come and visit your grave one day Dad. They both wanted to be at your funeral but we decided not to take them. They went off to school, and Sue and I dropped them off together, dressed like I was on my way to a funeral. I was.

Claire wasn't there at your funeral was she Dad, but for other reasons. Your daughter did not come to your funeral. How bad must things have between the two of you for that to happen?

She could have driven, she could have caught a taxi, reliable trains were available, I could have picked her up, dependable buses were around, other people would have gone out of their way to give her a lift, like the Robinsons who lived near her also in the lovely English county of Sussex but transport was not the cause of her absence.

She made a choice not to be at your funeral. Not good Brian, not good at all.

Perhaps I too should not have been there. I could have lived with that Dad in my own heart, quite easily.

Normal, what's normal? Well this was how normal came to be for us, for Claire, Nick and Brian Holbrook of 16 Manor Way.

Chapter 4 – Dark Clouds Gather

"Mum, is that you in the Dining Room?"

Too much drink can kill you

Mum was an alcoholic.

Audrey was an alcoholic.

And this time, I'm not talking about Audrey Hepburn.

She was dependant on regular consumption of alcoholic drink, to get by.

I feel utterly disloyal to you Mum for saying this of course, but it's just the truth isn't it?

I mean it is what happened after all isn't it, and how it was for years, isn't that right? I'm not imaging it, am I? Fabrication this is not, nor fiction.

Claire and I grew up with it as entirely normal, we grew up knowing no different than that it was perfectly standard for your Mum to be quite drunk at times, any day of the week, any month of the year, and as early on occasions as mid-morning. And we had become familiar with this normality from a very young age.

Mid-morning, a time in the day when perhaps a small coffee would actually have been more appropriate, more acceptable, more normal.

What the fuck did you do about it Dad?!

Why in God's name my father failed to challenge Mum on this, I will never, ever, ever know. As her husband he should have got this sorted in some way, he owed it to us as his children to do this, and when you consider that he was a family GP, professionally trained, at least to some extent in this illness, I can't really understand how he failed so badly to tackle it. It was staring him in the fucking face, every day, every morning, noon and night. He knew about it, he absolutely must have, and from very, very early on in their relationship too. It must have penetrated his nostrils as he woke up with Mum in bed, he must have seen how the level of the drinks bottles in the dining room downstairs kept going down and down, without convivial dinner parties being the cause of this particular reduction. He must have noticed that Mum's speech was the classically slurred speech of someone who was tipsy.

It would have been, and was, a constant shadow over the Holbrook family's life, all the time. Seven days a week, twelve months of every year. Quite simply for years.

"Seven by twenty four" is what we say these days isn't it?

He did try to my knowledge to "front it" on one occasion which I will tell you about very shortly, but he absolutely and categorically failed to sort it out.

And Boy, did it need sorting.
My Dad's failure even to address it lead to the series of events that you will now read about in this book. It resulted in a family of four being destroyed, as simple as that. As far as I can recall, and I don't know all of the conversations that he and Mum would have had over the years throughout their marriage, he utterly failed to recognise Mum's alcoholism.

He didn't wouldn't or couldn't look it in the eye. That was our Dad, this was what family meant to Claire and I. Somehow I can smell whisky now as I write.

There is good reason to believe that Mum had actually been drinking a lot, probably from as early as her late teens. I don't think that I can or will ever know what bad event happened in Mum's life up in Stockton-on-Tees, and if indeed that same event lead to her first drinking. Behold the cause and its dreadful effect.

When she and Dad met they were in the army after the war and I would guess that drinking in the evenings was probably a fully normal - (that word again) - and acceptable habit within that environment. I should think that it was quite encouraged to join the rest of the corps or whatever it was called for a drink or two at the end of the day.

Nice camouflage Mum. The Army is good at that, or so I hear.

How easy it must have been for her to drink what she needed to drink in that environment, quite unchallenged and in the very open. After all, everyone else was doing it! Couldn't have been easier! Like someone working in a cigarette factory in Cuba and smoking all day. Or someone in a chocolate factory nibbling at samples of fresh chocolate throughout the working day, just taking a small piece of chocolate from the monotonous grey conveyor belt, "only for quality purposes you understand."
It probably went by completely unnoticed. Dad liked a few beers I seem to remember him telling us but I don't think he was ever in danger of being dependent on drink in any way at all.

Unlike Mum. Very different. Different class of drinker. Different need you see.

Let me tell you now about the time that Dad challenged Mum, the one time to my certain knowledge that he did this. I know because I witnessed it. It must have happened thirty to thirty five years ago, and yet I remember it so very vividly. I know precisely which way the main characters were even facing at the time. Not because my mind is making it up, or distorting it, or deceiving me over time No, not that, really. I remember it because it must have been burned on my mind as soon as it happened.

I recall in detail exactly how I was positioned in the room in 16 Manor Way. It was a late summer evening, probably September time I would say. I would have been around eleven, making it something like 1972. Claire would have been ten, Mum around forty seven and Dad a little younger by two years. I had come down stairs into the dining room almost certainly because I had heard Mum down there. You see in 16 Manor Way, my bedroom was at the front over the dining room. Drive round there yourself one day to Blackheath in London SE3 9EF if you want to, and you'll see it immediately to the right as you look onto the house, above the ground floor dining room. That would be the dining room where the drinks cabinet was kept.

Quite a cabinet it was too, inherited by my Dad from his mother. It was a dark brown wooden cabinet, mahogany at least to look at, rather northern in its appeal, it made the whole room rather dark, perhaps in more ways than we knew at the time.

It would have lived for very many years "up North" in Grapenhall, a pleasant and affluent part of Warrington, before making the dubious journey down to 16 Manor Way, in the lovely leafy suburb of Blackheath, London SE3 9EF. As you went into the dining room, the brass light switch was up on the wall on your left, a little too high up for Claire and I when we were young!

And there too positioned hard up against the wall, was the drinks cabinet. It was generally well-stocked.

It wasn't just for drinks to be accurate as it had a large drawer that contained all sorts of crap in it. Napkins, both paper and linen, corkscrews of course, dinner table mats, pens and writing paper, Christmas wrapping paper, sellotape, some old medals, scissors, loads of very dark 1 penny and three-penny bit coins scattered throughout the drawer. It was a real mess, and I don't ever remember it being tidy, it always was a mess as far as I can look back. Good place to find things mind you like sellotape or scissors or wrapping paper of some description. And there a little down to the right-hand side of the cabinet, at about the level of your hip pocket, in a decidedly heavy and awkward drawer, very cleverly built, sturdy and durable, was the drinks section.

16 Manor Way

Deep. Dark. Black.

It always smelt of red wine, and I remember that it had a brass Lion's head handle on the front of it, with a dark green felt lining at the bottom inside. Probably the original lining too I wouldn't mind betting.

Now, here's the thing, the drinks corner unit scraped when it was opened. You couldn't help it, even if you lifted it very deliberately to prevent or lessen the noise in some way. The cabinet simply scraped! Fifty years or more of dark wood on wood. Nothing else downstairs in our house made that same noise. You might as well have rigged up a large red warning light marked "Mum's drinking !!" in my bedroom immediately upstairs, because as long as I was awake, I knew when that damned drinks cabinet was being opened. I also had a sad and consistent idea of who was opening it. Sadly, in those days, I didn't understand why, if I ever did of course.

On this particular late summer evening I had come downstairs as I had heard the drawer scrape, I knew what this meant and so I decided to come down to ask Mum what she was doing.

Picture an eleven-year old boy feeling the need to do that if you will. Maybe I was growing up more and had some innate sense that this was not right, that it was not good, and perhaps that more than that it was a very bad thing for our family, and that it needed to be tackled in some way. You can but hope. This was the only time that I can ever remember doing this. I was just eleven remember.

And just think please of this situation as I try to describe this to you, thirty five years after it actually happened. You might like to visualise it as a painting, or a photograph, or the picture of a film set. I can't really step back from it as I was one of the actors in this little tragedy.

Consider an elegant 1920s house in South London, overcast cool summer evening, lady in her forties secretly swigging whisky directly from the glass bottle, believing that no-one knew that she was in there. In walks a young boy who simply wanted nothing more than that his Mum would stop drinking.

I would never want our children to go through anything like the experience I had that evening.

Mum hurriedly tried to put the beige tin cap back onto the scotch bottle as she heard me coming down the stairs, and to get it back into the drinks unit. But that old scraping wood was having none of it, and as she rushed the bottle back into the cabinet, the wood made its instantly recognisable noise, and the numerous bottles clanked against each other harshly. Rumbled. Then I was in the dining room with Mum, standing on the deep rich cream carpet, trying to understand what she was doing. I looked at Mum, she looked down at me, and wiped her mouth with the back of her right hand guiltily, but she knew that I knew.

Oh she knew. She had been caught hadn't she? And she didn't want to be caught or seen or found out. Who would?

I asked her what she was doing, and she made something up about getting some birthday card out of the drawer. Yeah, right, must have been one hell of a big card.

Dad then came in, I think he must have heard us talking from the dining room, perhaps he thought it was a little strange that I was up when I should have been asleep. He came into the dining room from the subdued light of the pine green hallway.

This must have been so very painful for Mum to have been caught drinking both by her husband and by her young son. Dad got very angry. You have to totally understand here that Brian Holbrook did this very rarely indeed. But I remember it. He seemed to know very clearly what had been going on here, and then he reached into the drinks cabinet and took out the whisky bottle. He was as angry as I ever saw him in our lives together.

By now, Mum was very upset – upset, emotional and drunk in our dark green dining room. The three stuffed brown trout in the Cooper bow-fronted case looking down from the wall to the right must have seen all of this going on in great detail. Dad then took the whisky bottle out and then did an amazing thing, amazing in that he would never do anything like this that I can remember ever again. He showed both Mum and I that he had put a mark on the level of drink in the bottle with a thick marker pen in bottle green I remember it clearly. Bottle green it had to be of course. Mum was so anxious and upset now.

"You've been drinking again Audrey haven't you?!" Dad said in a challenging tone.

Mum denied it.

Dad's voice was raised, so very unusual for him. Mum was crying more now, and Dad said that he knew where the marker was on the bottle and that the level had gone down.

"I marked it Audrey, I marked it!" he barked.

Mum denied it, again.

Dad was angry, nearly out of control, and noisy. I asked Mum again why she had been drinking and through her tears and fear she said that she hadn't, again. Dad then shouted at the top of his voice the words that I don't think that I will ever forget –

"For Christ's sake woman, can't you see the boy's worried sick? He's worried sick!"

Those words were burned into my head instantly, and they go with me to my grave. To my grave do you hear? For they are words that have an unstoppable power, a power to cut through time and take me in an instant back to the front room of 16 Manor Way.

Mum and Dad then left the room, Mum very distressed and drunk. They went to talk, I guess. I can't imagine that the conversation, if you can call it that, would have been easy.

The scene closes then as the eleven year-old boy then leaves the dark room that was our dining room, presumably climbed the stairs on his own, got into his bed, lay there confused and in need of explanation, somehow went to sleep, and in true Brian Holbrook tradition that evening's incident was never, ever discussed again.

Not once. Can you believe it? Not once. Nice one Dad, GP Dad.

Fuck.

It's interesting what can be found on the web about the effects that alcoholic drinking has on children. Here's an example, this is from the THE ADULT CHILDREN EDUCATIONAL FOUNDATION, and it's called "CHILDREN LEARN WHAT THEY LIVE":

If a child lives with criticism,
  She learns to condemn.
If a child lives with hostility,
  He learns to fight.
If a child lives with ridicule,
  She learns to be shy.
If a child lives with shame,
  He learns to feel guilty.
If a child lives with tolerance,
  She learns to be patient.
If a child lives with encouragement,
  He learns confidence.
If a child lives with praise,
  She learns to appreciate.
If a child lives with fairness,

He learns justice.
If a child lives with security,
  She learns to have faith.
If a child live with approval,
  He learns to like himself.
If a child lives with acceptance and friendship,
  He learns to find love in the world.

The thing about drinking in the Holbrook family, such as it was, is that it really was this "Huge Elephant in the drawing room". You've heard of this notion before right ?, - the idea that there is something large and highly significant in your room but which bizarrely never gets spoken about, acknowledged, or even referred to. We all see it, we all walk round it, it's just there, we can all point to it, like you would do to a real elephant, and yet no-one says

"Hang on a moment, that's an elephant isn't it? What the hell's it doing in middle of our drawing room?!"

It never, ever gets spoken about, over years of time together.

So in our case, we had Mum drinking on and off, more on than off, throughout our childhood and this was never discussed within the family. What has come to light over the years since Mum took her life in 1980 was that our family friends knew that she drank, you could smell it on her breath when she was close, all too often.

One of Mum's very dearest and most loyal friends Anne Wood said that Mum once called her on the telephone, I guess to chat on the phone, over twenty times in just one single afternoon. Twenty separate calls from the same person!! What must Anne have thought about this?

Also married to John a popular GP, perhaps she actually had a very clear idea of what illness Mum had. Maybe if she had been given a chance to talk to Mum that would have made a difference, who knows? Anne is a super person, and she just might have had some effect. But there again, as Mum said to Betty Hitchcock, many years ago, "Some things you never talk about .." so maybe not.

Betty was a very close friend to Mum, and knew that not all was well. Her question to Mum one evening which had prompted the reply above was this, in good Midlands fashion I have to comment too:

"What ails thee Audrey?"

Long, long pause followed by "Some things you never talk about".

I can't tell you why Mum needed to drink alcohol. Actually I can, she had become dependent on it of course that's why she needed to consume it regularly. Rather, I can't tell you why she started it in the first place. Did she start in an attempt to rub something out of her mind, had she gone through a trauma that she needed to somehow lessen or even to make disappear through alcohol? Did drink make her feel good and help her to begin to forget something bad that had happened to her? We "knew" that Mum's own Mum had died when Mum was in her early teens. We never ever spoke about her parents as we grew up. I do clearly remember Dad telling us this detail just once, that Mum's father had re-married a women that Mum never liked.

Gosh, imagine that Dad.
Quite a thought eh? Just think of the effect of that on the children. Wow.

Dad had an idea, (for once, it really didn't happen that often), that Mum had joined up as a nurse at the age of eighteen as this got her out of the home at the earliest possible opportunity and gave here some financial independence. Maybe you were right Dad.

16 Manor Way

She didn't stay in contact with her father or step-mother as far as Claire and I understood and we never grew up having met either of them … as far as I knew. I have it in my mind that Mum's Dad lived a long time, certainly until Claire and I were into our teens.

I wonder what conversations were had with us as young kids that we never grew up talking about Mum's parents. I don't remember it occurring even once. How could our early thoughts as young kids have been managed so successfully that I never even asked Mum when her Mum or her Dad died.
Or how? I don't believe that I can even tell you what their first names were. This saddens me greatly. So many questions and so few answers.

This weekend just gone by, there was a picture of my lovely wife Sue as a young girl in a school uniform, on the mantel piece of her parents' house in Crowcombe, Somerset.
It was in colour and Sue would have been about ten years old I would guess. As we were looking at it, Sophie our daughter said "You look funny Mummy, funny hairstyle!"

How really wonderful that Sophie and Jack will grow up knowing all these kind of things about their Mum, with quite a lot of pictures of both of their parents at different points in time in their lives. Claire and I never had any pictures of Mum as a kid, at all. Not one. Zero pictures. They must have been taken. I'd give a hundred thousand pounds to have a picture of Mum when she was at school. Don't care what her hairstyle is like. Just a picture of Mum as a young girl, please, that's all. Not much to ask is it?

Mum was a nurse in the Queen Alexander's Nursing Corps. She sounded like she was very good too. Dad told me that she was chosen, along with some others, to nurse some British officers who had been badly burnt in an exercise in a barn, somewhere in Germany I seem to remember. This must have been after the War, I don't know when exactly. I wonder where those officers are now if indeed they are still alive.

Mum formed a great friendship in the QA s with my godmother, Betty Hitchcock. They worked and travelled together over quite a few years, and later when Mum was married with our "family", Betty would visit us at weekends and spend summer holiday time with us. She was and has always been a truly great friend to the Holbrooks.

We saw Betty recently up at her house in Nottingham, she was in rude health as they say. Sue, Jack, Sophie and I all went to see here at her house on the outskirts of the city that's in the middle of England, not too far away from where I was born in Worksop. Betty made us a good strong cup of tea and brought us in some biscuits and pieces
of fruit cake. Dad liked that very much, it was always a favourite of his, that and Marks and Spencer Custard Tarts.

I asked Betty why she thought that Mum drank alcohol, and she told me something interesting. She said that one particular evening she had taken the courage to ask Mum this same question when they were nurses together.

At what she considered to be the appropriate moment, in her fine and direct Nottingham way, Betty asked Mum these exact words. She said

"Audrey, what ails thee?"

Mum had looked away for quite a long time, in silence, and then suddenly turned her gaze back at Betty and replied darkly, "There are some things that you just never talk about, never".

End of conversation.

Another short drama now follows

Stage Direction - enter the character of Alcoholism into the Holbrook's lives, stage left.

Stays on stage throughout the play, until the final scene.

END OF PLAY. ALL GO HOME.

The following are some of the characteristics, agreed upon by one Alanon-Acoa group, of children who have grown up with one or more alcoholic parents.

They found that these things resulted:

a. They became isolated and afraid of people and authority figures;

b. They became approval seekers and lost our identity in the process;

c. They are frightened by angry people and any personal criticism;

d. They either become alcoholics, marry them, or both, or find another compulsive personality such as a workaholic to fulfill our sick abandonment needs;

e. They live life from the viewpoint of victims and are attracted by that weakness in their love and friendship relations;

f. They have an overdeveloped sense of responsibility and it is easier for them to be concerned with others rather than themselves. This enables them not to look too closely at their faults.

g. They get guilt feelings when they stand up for themselves instead of giving in to others;

h. They became addicted to excitement;

i. They confuse love and pity and tend to "love" people they can "pity" and "rescue";

j. They have stuffed their feelings from their traumatic childhoods and have lost the ability to feel or express their feelings because it hurts so much; (DENIAL)

k. They judge themselves harshly and have a very low sense of self-esteem;

l. They are dependent personalities who are terrified of abandonment and will do anything to hold on to a relationship in order not to experience painful abandonment feelings which we received from living with sick people who were never there emotionally for us;

m. Alcoholism is a family disease and they became Para-alcoholics and took on the characteristics of that disease even though they did not pick up the drink;

n. Para-alcoholics are reactors rather than actors.

I would very much like to pick up on some of these observations above in some detail, as they related to my sister Claire and me. The points B C and K were particularly true of Claire and me. Over the years, Mum's drinking crushed the life out of our self-confidence, it smashed our sense of identity, and directly gave us both a strong tendency to run away from things rather than stand up for ourselves. Being adopted will have contributed to this partially too I am very sure, but in the same way that Dad failed to stand up to Mum's tragic addiction, so that same flaw was developed in both of us. It applies to me to this very day, aged forty eight. Given the choice to stand and fight, or to leave it, I'll pursue the second strategy thank you very much. I'm quite brilliant at it, beaten into second place only by Claire. That's me on the edge, steadily stepping to one side, ever so deftly, away from the main party, often unnoticed at the time.

It's simply fascinating isn't it to see how one member of a family who has an addiction, can have such a deep effect on the other family members. I don't know fully the mechanics of it, I just don't understand how it all works when you have a regular drinker in your family, but nevertheless Claire and I both very definitely developed steadily into people who felt very isolated, and who just got on with what he had to get on with.

Head above water.

Reasonable survival.

Existence.

I think it must have gone something like this:

Bad event in Mum's life > The cement is now very wet > Mum starts drinking > Becomes addicted to alcohol quickly by her twenties > Mum marries > Can't have her own children > Has greater access to alcohol while her husband is at work > Is unchallenged and drinks more and more regularly > Her dependency increases further > Adopted children (all 3) arrive > Father does nothing about Mother's drinking even now > Situation of drunk mother becomes totally normal for the growing children > The children withdraw into themselves over their childhood to get away from drunk mother > Father at work long hours and does not address situation still now, or chooses to avoid it > Kids become islands emotionally by age six or seven probably, that's how they cope with the nightmare at home > Kids grow up with it being normal not to tackle hugely important issue > All too late to go back and undo patterns > Mother kills herself > Even further withdrawal occurs > One fucking huge mess > The cement is now totally dry.

I simply can not tell you how utterly miserable I was in my mid-twenties, a few years after Mum had killed herself and Dad had re-married. In 1987 specifically, when I was twenty six. You just don't want to know how low my level of self-esteem was then. We're taking horizontal okay? Nothing showing on the radar. Only my sense of humour and regular masturbation got me through it. Those skills and the fact that I was fortunate enough to have a great job as a secondary-school teacher, all that I had really ever wanted to do for a job. I loved being a teacher and the warming feel of a good school community, I always believed that it was something special.

Perhaps also because we were adopted, we had an additional and very confused sense of identity, of who we really were, where we were from, and why we found ourselves where we did. Point B above applied to the both of us for sure. Do you know, as Claire and I grew up, if we ever did, I don't think that either of us got real validation from Mum that we really were wanted and loved and part of the family. I just don't remember it. We did at times from Dad, I remember that very clearly, but not from Mum. It all seemed a little less enthusiastic than it might have been. I am sure that I would remember it if it had taken place regularly. I don't remember the big, unequivocal hugs, the times of great laughter, the endless love. I don't remember them Mum. You seemed to be a little on the edge, not quite taking part fully. Perhaps she had more than enough going on in her own head to cope with.

As per point K above, both Claire and I had deeply low self-esteem. The source for me was a particular combination of my adoption and Mum's alcoholism, in Claire's case she got three for the price of two and had I'm sure a level of depression thrown in too, just for good measure. I can't say it more clearly than that can I? More noticeably, Claire and I both grew up being very independent people. We would both take, and indeed need, very substantial amounts of time on our own. Claire would spend many hours as a young girl, right into her teens, in her bedroom at the top of 16 Manor Way. I don't know what she did up there, - reading, writing, drawing sometimes, painting, school homework perhaps. No convenient mobile phones or metallic pink iPods invented in those days for her to play with. However, she seemed very happy in her own company …. or perhaps what I should rather say is that she spent lots of time up there on her own, because they are two different things aren't they? They are very different things of course.

I wonder where our Mum was for Claire all that time, when the ten-year old girl was two floors above alone in her room, and Mum was making the dark wooden drinks cabinet produce that tell-tale scraping noise I shouldn't wonder. Sorry Mum, but that's how it was so often for us. True.

There were actually periods of time when Mum didn't drink. I can distinctly remember when I was fourteen or fifteen coming home from school for many weeks, perhaps even months, and being so pleased and happy inside that Mum had not been drinking. I never said that anyone of course, why would I? But I remember it well. It was nice. She would smile, and we would have normal conversations. There was no smell of drink on her breath. We would all sit down and have tea together. Dad would be out until about eight pm doing his evening surgery but the three of us, Mum, Claire and I would have some nice time together. Almost normal I guess you could say. Claire would then go up to her room of course, and I would go off and do the mountains of homework that I had to do. Funny how I just got on with all of those essays, projects, test papers and so on. That's the independence coming through again you see, head down, grinding away, never mind thinking about why we're doing this. I became very adept at banging my head against a wall only because it's so nice when you stop!

I would come down and see Dad when he came home from his surgery, and then go back upstairs to my room. Dad used to call Mum "Lovey" when he came in, I remember that very clearly on many occasions. I think that they had loved each other. I hope that's true. I have few good memories of them loving each other in front of me. The "lovey" moment in the hallway I do remember well.

So that's what I wanted to tell you about Mum, about her alcohol addiction, her denial, and the wine-stained scraping wooden drinks cabinet of 16 Manor Way. For years after Mum died, I didn't drink beer or wine. I had an aversion to alcohol of all types, and in particular to any advertising on the television for alcoholic drink. I didn't like seeing the Gordon's gin adverts or the Martini adverts in the cinema either, I must have looked a little different sitting there in the cinema closing my eyes and refusing to watch the ads for alcoholic drinks. I resented them, and more significantly I knew just how different the reality of alcoholism had been for our family than it was for the glamorous, young, sexy people sitting on board a yacht in the slick cinema advertisement. I remember going with some friends to see a James Bond 007 film at the Odeon in Eltham, (nice juxtaposition don't you think, James Bond and Eltham?), and feeling very angry about an advert that was running then for Gordon's Gin. It was a sexy, glamorous commercial of course and I wanted to stand up and shout aloud …

"Look what it did to my Mum everyone, you really don't want to touch this stuff, I've seen what it really does to you, and to those around you. Stick to milk, it's much more natural, and less dangerous!"

In the Princess of Wales pub up in Blackheath, I did used to drink milk rather than beer. I quite liked it actually, and still do. I drink no alcohol now.

Of course, a few words here don't illuminate the terrible effects of alcoholism. But perhaps you can see from our story the stages in the process that were being set in place as a result of Mum's drinking. It all had a sense of Fate and of being plain unstoppable, and of having a strong momentum of its own. I have no illusions at all that for Dad to have helped Mum's alcohol addiction was easy. I actually don't know Dad that you could have turned it round, not unless you had been there at source with her in her teens. I am still deeply saddened when I think of Mum falling over on a step in a fishing tackle shop in Lewisham early one Saturday afternoon, tipsy again.

Embarrassing, awkward, it wasn't like that in the Gordon's cinema advertisement now was it, I don't recall anyone slipping or falling there. They all seemed to be in very strong control, even the clean-shaven handsome one steering the yacht so skillfully with one hand! Amazing.

I sit here almost frozen with pain when I visualize my sister Claire finding half-filled bottles of Johnnie Walker whisky in the laundry basket, and under the bed in the spare room.

What the fuck were they doing there Mum?

Why the fuck did you not attempt to sort this out Dad?

Was this normal in a family, and why did Mum do this?

Claire came up to me in my bedroom one afternoon and asked me her brother, why the bottles were there, but I couldn't help her. You see, she was nine at the time and I was ten. What did I know, what could I say, how was I going to answer her when I wanted the same questions answered? I have a feeling that it was through moments like this that the damage to people around the drinker starts. Something makes me feel that you are deeply hurt and confused by it, but because it doesn't get talked about, let alone addressed, it stays inside you and begins to eat away.

Does that make any sense? Take that afternoon when Claire and I were talking about the whisky bottle in the linen basket, that little scene would have ended with Claire putting the whisky bottle back into the linen basket, me carrying on with whatever I was doing (probably homework), and then no more being said. Dad and Mum probably never knew that Claire had even found it, but we as kids would have paid for that little discovery by hurting inside.

That was nearly forty years ago, but I remember like it was just yesterday, such was its impression on me.

Sorry Claire, I might have helped you more that afternoon.

Chapter 5 – "Oh my God, she's killed herself!"

This I never understood

The Audi 200, a luxurious German executive saloon, was in metallic silver I seem to remember, and staring up at me from the glossy pages of the Sunday magazine. I am sitting on the left-hand side of the table as you look out into our long back garden at 16 Manor Way. It's a Sunday morning, it is the 15th November in 1980. I'm in a towelling dressing gown, eating toast and drinking tea about 8 am, reading the Sunday papers. Picture all of this happening in a nice middle-class house in Blackheath, London SE3 9EF. It is a very bright, sunny November morning, rather nice actually. Or at least it has been nice for the first hour or so that I have been up.

I was looking at the Audi in the glossy Sunday magazine… that's what I was doing twenty five years ago when I heard Dad shout down from the very top of the house –

"Oh my God, she's killed herself".

More words that burned into me for life.

I didn't know it at the time, as we were all about to go into a powerful whirlwind of so many emotions, but hearing those words just the once, was enough to burn them into my mind for ever.

FOR EVER

I think it's the context that does that to you. The situation that you are in at the time. And that particular context for me was what happened on that bright, sunny Sunday morning in November of 1980.

16 Manor Way

How long he'd been in the room I don't know. Had he seen her for some time lying in the bed? Probably not. I think Dad had gone upstairs to take Mum a cup of tea. You see Mum had killed herself by placing a plastic bag over her head and suffocating herself.

A large, black plastic bag that "obstructed her upper airways", that's what it read on her death certificate. "She killed herself", it also said, in spidery black handwriting right in the middle of box 6 on the Death Certificate where the Cause of Death is entered.

A little disrespectful I thought, he might have written "Mrs Holbrook killed herself", or "Audrey took her own life", or "Doctor Holbrook's wife took her own life". However, what happened, was that she did indeed take her own life. Our beloved Mum killed herself. She committed suicide, as we say.

She also chose to leave us, if that's what she knew she was doing. To leave us for ever.

The precise sequence of events is not clear to me, whilst certain details remain as familiar and as memorable in my mind as if they had happened just this very morning.

If I had been filmed, I guess that in slow motion you'd have seen me leaving the table at great speed and running out of the breakfast room to go upstairs.
Mum's body (now) was in the spare room at the top of the house, at the front looking out into Manor Way, two long storeys below. Mum was already on her way to Heaven you see.

I don't remember going up the stairs, at all.

Did I run up there as fast as I could? Did I go up briskly? Did I in fact just walk up there normally? Don't remember, don't know.

I think that Claire my sister got to see her first after Dad, and before me. Claire's bedroom you see was at the top of our two storey house next to the spare room where Mum had slept that night. I believe that she had slept there that particular night as Dad "had been snoring a lot recently". Hmmm, I wonder. Dad did have some breathing difficulties when sleeping, associated I think with an inner ear infection that he got from time to time. He had experienced this since a young boy, originally as a result of swimming pool water getting into his ear. It seemed to come and go over the years that I knew him. Not the ear, the illness.

So, our Mum and Dad had slept in separate rooms that night. Bit like Her Majesty the Queen and Prince Phillip, or so we hear. There's more to that comparison actually than might first appear, as Dad looked very like HRH Prince Phillip. Or rather as I liked to think to myself as a kid, Prince Phillip looked a lot like my Dad. Slightly taller, otherwise very alike. I think HRH had a bigger house, several titles, more servants, lots of land, the odd piece of historical jewellery, and faster cars, while my Dad, well you see he had an alcoholic wife.

Perhaps their marriage, like all marriages, was going through poor times. Don't know.

Dad must have gone into the spare room and "seen the scene". There can't have been much to take in, can there? You open the door to the bedroom, I guess that you go in quietly in case your partner is still asleep. Maybe you're thinking of drawing the curtains as you approach the door, mug of tea in the off-door hand, and looking ahead to what you're going to do that day. Perhaps the black floral curtains weren't drawn that night, although they were certainly open when I ran into the room that black and sunny morning. We'd often go into Greenwich Park at the weekend to take our dogs Pip and Tessa for a walk, perhaps those pictures were going through my Dad's head. Or something else.

Anyway, if they were, or if some completely different images and thoughts were in his head as he opened the door, it opened to the right, they would have surely been obliterated in an instant. Your still (in both senses) sleeping Partner has something over their head. Your eyes tell you that it's not normal. I would guess that my Dad's brain also told him in the briefest of moments possible

"Don't be silly, it's only the blanket, or a hot water bottle, or the blue sleeping bag, or her dressing gown",

but then as you go across to the bed you can see what the thing is, and it's what you thought it was when you first saw it, the very thing that you didn't want it to be, for that would be a catastrophic event for our family, for their relationship however it was, for his reputation as a family GP, for the kids, for everyone.

"No it can't be, it will be something else completely different when I get to the side of the bed, you'll see, really, probably just the blanket ….."

But no.

Any light that was coming through those dark flowered curtains that we had in that room at the top of 16 Manor Way would have made that plastic bag shine a little.

Blankets don't do that, blankets don't shine! – sleeping bags neither, at least not like that - nor does light make the surface of a towelling dressing gown shimmer. It's a plastic bag. It really is! I knew it as soon as I saw it.

Nothing wrong at all with Brian Holbrook's eye sight in those days.

I wonder where the cup of tea was by now, don't you? In Dad's hand still …? Hard to think of Dad putting it down carefully isn't it, so as not to spill it on the carpet when he was having to deal with what was in front of him… up in the spare room.

I think his priorities had just been re-decided for him, in a split second, as he entered the spare room on that bright, sunny November morning in 1980.

It was a cold winter's day I remember, and our Mum was now cold too.

Audrey Hepburn, Audrey Holbrook. Cold.

We never spoke about those moments, as far as I recall, even twenty five years later.

I hope that he rushed over there, and pulled the bag from Mum's face, from the face of his wife.

Perhaps he leapt over the second single bed up in our spare room like he'd never had to do before, his body taking over in a desperate attempt to drag the bag from her in case she'd only just done it.

Yes, maybe we'll be okay, perhaps she's still alive, maybe she's only just done this and I can get to her. As a GP, taking her pulse, and feeling for any breath coming from her mouth, they would both have come naturally to him. Yet, it must have been the hardest occasion that this GP ever had to look for a still beating pulse, that of his wife. Perhaps he didn't even do that. Maybe it was clearly not worth it. Did Claire and I go through his thoughts at this stage I wonder?

No pulse, no breath, only the cold of Death.

England, a sunny Sunday morning in the month of November 1980.

I think that you went into that room Claire before me didn't you? I never saw Mum with the plastic bag on her face, in fact I don't think I ever saw the plastic bag. Actually, perhaps that's not true, perhaps I had in fact seen it several times but down in the kitchen in a small cardboard package with several other black plastic bags, the box marked "12 Waitrose Quality Black Bin Liners – with plastic ties". Maybe it had been in our lives for several weeks before carrying out a purpose for which Waitrose had never intended it. It probably had, until late that night in November 1980.

What I do remember very clearly, is being calm. I remember it absolutely.

Completely calm.

Totally so.

Absolutely calm.

No shock whatsoever. None.

I was nineteen, my mother had just killed herself, and I was calm. My father had just found my mother dead through suffocation in our spare room, and I was calm.

Quite calm.

I have no recollection of shock, of surprise, of nerves, or of anger, resentment, bitterness, guilt, fear, or feeling sick.

Only of being absolutely calm.

As calm as could be, in fact.

I said to Dad

"Don't worry Dad, we'll get through this and get you fishing again soon".
I remember it very clearly. How nice was I that in that situation I was thinking about him. He said nothing back to us by way of explanation. I wonder why.

I phoned the police, how exciting I get to dial 999, don't think I had ever done that before until that bright, sunny November morning, and they had come round quickly.

I wasn't there when they arrived. I had calmly gone round to see Anne and John Wood who lived two doors away at 20 Manor Way. Anne and John were really super friends to our family, with four children of their own, three girls Annette, Nichola and Monica, and their son, my best friend, Matthew. Mind you, I wouldn't have minded being friends with their middle daughter Nichola, but that's a story for another time! Matthew is a year younger than me, and we shared the same birthday on January 5th – naff time of year to have a birthday believe me!

I must have got dressed and walked up and out of the drive and turned right to No 20. Don't think I even cleaned my teeth. I walked round there, very calmly.

John was a GP too, like so many of our family friends from the medical profession. Anne was a qualified nurse, and they generally drove Renaults. Their French cars would have been on their drive that morning I'm sure, as I walked calmly across the red tarmac drive that dropped down slightly down towards their front door.

Anne answered, and she knew something was wrong.

I felt very empowered with being the carrier of this news, and still I was calm.

So calm.

There was no shaking, no crying as you might expect, only a calm messenger.
I can only say that I experienced no surprise at what was being played out. Somehow, and I don't understand this, it was like it was not a shock. Perhaps my relationship with Mum had been broken down totally by that time.

We talked at the door a little, and I think I went into the warm of the Wood's house which I had come to know as a second home over so many happy years. Normal years too actually, in parallel with those not normal years, the same ones in fact running alongside each other with exactly the same numbers and dates on them, yet so very different.

To the right, was the distinctive wood-panelled sitting room, host to several marvellous games of Charades at Christmas time, parties that I never wanted to leave. Christmas tree in the window, the lights reflected on the glass of the French doors, the warm metallic gas fire in the wall on the right, the two big sofas, and Christmas cards and decorations flowing around the panelled walls at a height that a young kid could not reach them, deliberate of course. And always, always, a large tin of Quality Street chocolates, which I came to like over the years. I always liked the yellow toffee ones from Party No.1, and then the chocolate and toffee, and then some of those brightly foil-wrapped ones, that had such strange things inside them, that strangely seemed to become okay to eat over the years, resulting in me, can you believe this, actually liking those elegant and distinctively-shaped green diamond chocolates, with whatever is inside them?!

God Bless Quality Street, tasting so good at No.20 Manor Way. Wood-panelled Christmas Parties at 20 Manor Way, Blackheath SE3, terrific. God Bless you Anne and John, and Nichola too of course. X

By the time that I had got back home to no.16, the cops were there. Forgive me, I can't recollect the cars or vans, like something the Sweeney drove in those days I guess. Rover, Allegro, Ford Transit, maybe the Allegro with the square steering wheel? Or a John Thaw/Dennis Waterman Ford Granada, classic cop car that. We had one, in white actually – SLT 966L - went to collect it with Dad from Fry's of Lewisham one day, - black leather interior, automatic, classic simple lines. Not as cool as the Capri of course, but that would have been a little too risky for a GP to go around in wouldn't it?

I remember one policeman in uniform, now up in the spare room, looking at me quite suspiciously, and I think he was suspicious of me because I was so calm.

Totally calm.

Not a hint of shock.

I wasn't crying, I wasn't shaking or visibly upset in any way. Plain calm, a calm nineteen year old boy whose mother has just died, and you're not impacted by that in any way son…. Hmm. Maybe it was all too soon, maybe he's seen it before. Anyway, I remember him looking at me, holding his gaze into my eyes, and me turning away.

"I didn't do it Mr Regan, honest, I didn't really, I ain't lying - ask anyone round here, they'll tell you… she topped herself, the Doctor's wife topped herself".

And she had.

That's exactly what she had done. That bright, sunny, November Sunday morning.

Audi 200.

Anne and John.

Our Mum, in 16 Manor Way.

Chapter 6 – Let the Destruction Begin

"I'm taking it all back, and now"!

It's always going to be hard when one of your separated (or widowed) parents starts to see someone else for the first time, isn't it? Our image of our Mum and Dad is largely defined by them being with the other partner isn't it? They are two halves of the same whole aren't they? As we live with them, we watch how they interact with each other. We listen to the things that they say, what they agree on, or not on some occasions. We've always known them together, they're two halves of the same whole, Mum and Dad. The clue is to be found in the word "and", it's what we can call a joining word.

For a child who has lost one parent, seeing the surviving parent starting to be with a new friend is particularly tough isn't it? It might actually be more than tough, it might be plain shocking. There is a sense of moving on, of going onto something new and unknown, but for a young child that something can only be founded on sheer disloyalty to the parent who is here no more.

My parents were not divorced as you know, but I imagine that for children whose parents have separated or gone on to divorce, this must be equally hard. We would always hope that in the case of separation, the children can at least see both parents from time to time, but the reality is that it will be hard of course. Perhaps that situation comes with its very own kind of pain. I am quite sure that it does. Two houses, alternate Sunday lunches, maybe two different bedrooms to have, fun!

Yes but not really, because of one on-going pain.

In the case of my father Brian, I first became aware of him seeing someone else after Mum had died, in the spring of 1983. I had been away in Spain for a few months, having graduated in "MILARS". Oh, what's MILARS you ask? "Modern Iberian and

99

Latin-American Regional Studies". There, now you know! It was an Arts degree in Spanish with elements of Language, History, Literature and Politics from both Spain and South America. I took this at University College London from 1979-1982.

Having graduated with a 2:2 degree in the summer of 1982, I knew that I wanted to go into Teaching. It was really the only thing that I ever wanted to do, I had a vocation I guess. I've got an Audi now, but I had a vocation then. I had got a place from the University of Sheffield to take a Post-Graduate Certificate in Education (PGCE) from September 1983 onwards, and so I took a year off. This seems very normal now doesn't it, to have a "Gap Year" and go off up the Amazon (not the bookstore, the river) and "find yourself"! I don't quite remember all of the details now, but as I recall they did not have a place for me at Sheffield in the 1982-1983 programme and so that's why I took a year out. Seemed like a good idea at the time, it made solid sense, right kind of thing to do.

I knew that I needed to improve my Spanish still further and so I made some investigations in how I could go across to Spain for some time, earn some money, and come back to England some time later with much-improved Spanish. It was already pretty good, but not fluent enough if I was really going to be strong at teaching it to GCSE and A Level.

It was something that I am very proud of, that I made myself go to Spain for several months on my own. You might think that was no Big Deal, but this was just two years after Mum had killed herself and believe me when I say that our family was "all at sea". Actually, the reality that I can see with great clarity now was that we were three individuals all dealing with Audrey's suicide in three different ways.

Claire, now studying Art at Goldsmith's college in New Cross in South London, dealt with it by taking herself off to her room for lengthy periods on her own, on most evenings as I remember.

Meet Island No.1.

I got on with my life by working through my university course as best I could and through having a great holiday job as a Ward Orderly at Greenwich District Hospital. Mum had found me that job when I was in the Lower 6th at school, and it was without doubt one of the best things that I ever did. It was probably the perfect antidote to my privileged education at Westminster Public School. Thanks Mum, maybe you did love me.

Say hi to Island No. 2.

Quite how Dad the Greenwich GP dealt with Mum's death I'm unsure. I remember him commenting to me on the day that she died, "People will think things about me". What I am sure about is that he "got over" her quite soon. Or perhaps I am being totally unfair to him and he never did. No, I reckon he did. A third possibility is quite definitely that in fact he just didn't deal with it at all, that he never really handled it. He might just have parked the whole damn thing in his head, "drawn a line under it" as he would say, which was really code for something else.

Meet Island No.3.

I don't remember him being counselled in any way, or talking about this alien concept of us meeting with a qualified counsellor at any point. He was literally surrounded by medical professionals, geographically and in his working life, surely several people would have suggested this to him, if not for him then for us his hurting children? I do remember one Christmas time very clearly, not long after Mum had died, so it would have been either in 1981 or 1982, and in December strangely enough. This was before Dad had met the monster, or at least I think it was. He may have been seeing the woman who would become his second wife while Mum was alive. On this particular evening, with our Christmas tree set up and decorated in the sitting room, (we always had a real tree I remember), I had just burst into tears and had gone into the warmth and security of the familiar sitting room. Dad was finishing off a phone call and Claire was not upstairs on this occasion as I remember. I think she was watching the television downstairs.

Dad had seen me cry and came into the room after his call, and we sat there on the brown sofa and cried together and talked a little. We were still mates then I think, I do think so.

"I don't understand why Mum's gone Dad, why did she kill herself?"

"I don't think we'll ever know that Nick, she wasn't well, in her head. But she loved you very much, both you and Claire ".

Hhmm, right. Yes.
"Why didn't she talk with us? Tell us what was worrying her, we could have understood it and worked through it with her I'm sure".

"She had a lot of sadness in her that we don't really understand".

We talked and cried for quite some time, and the silver tinsel on the tree moved a little with the warmth of the central heating.

Please remember that we weren't coming to terms with our Mum having died of natural causes, although suffocation with a plastic bag is kind of natural I guess you could say. Mum had taken her own life, very suddenly for all of us, as far as I know. It came to be a totally shocking thing for Claire and I at eighteen and nineteen, a huge and terrifying meteor that came out of the dark, absolutely unseen. I don't think it was expected by Dad, but who quite knows. Mum had been an alcoholic for as long as Claire and I could remember, and probably Dad too. A final further detail, just for the record, Claire and I weren't exactly Mr. and Miss Personally Confident of 1961 and 1962, being adopted that is, and so we needed our own time to adjust to Mum's suicide.

This was of course precisely the time when we should all have been having counselling of some kind with a trained professional. Should have known that one Dad, you being a medical man.

But then again, perhaps you didn't want something to come out?

16 Manor Way

Looking back now on this time, Claire, Nick and Brian were three distinct islands moving apart in the ocean, and doing so very steadily. Yes, we were all based out of the same house, but we were dealing with our family's events in our own way with a distance between the three of us growing each week. We coped by surviving on our own. Mum's death had begun to separate us, but we were still friends I am sure at that point. It's just that Dad should have held us together, and pulled us back in, kept us together at all costs. He didn't of course.

Wanker.

I needed some kind of stability from somewhere and going off to a strange new place like Spain was at best a risk. It was quite brave of me to head off when I didn't want to go, but I knew that it was the right thing to do, and so off I went to Spain. I had a job through the CBEVE, the London-based "Central Bureau for Educational Visits and Exchanges". I remember the letters that I had from a Mr Anthony Howick. A group of us flew down to Malaga in Andalucia in January of 1983, and then went off to our various schools and colleges in the region. Mine was called el Colegio de San Jose, in a little village called Campillos. This would translate into something like "LittleField" in English, and indeed there were many pretty poppy-filled fields around there. However, what I had not been told by Mr Howick was that the school was an institution for boys with behavioural and discipline problems. They had come from all over Spain to this school, it was a boarding establishment, and they were not allowed out of the school's buildings. There were guards I suppose you might call them at the front door at all times, and the security was tight. Nice.

I could come and go as I wanted and I would go out running up the lane several evenings a week, with the inmates shouting through the windows at me something probably very rude and actually very funny in Spanish. Good Luck to them, they had tough backgrounds. I wasn't the only one of course.

My room was as white as you could imagine, and there was a reason for that.

I was in "la enfermeria", the infirmary. It had been specially prepared for me in white paint, - floor, walls and ceiling, it wasn't particularly large, it was very clean and light, and did I mention how white it was? Dazzlingly so!

You can probably tell that I was not very happy there. The school's staff were all actually very friendly, and at break-time, the prison doors would open to us and were given the temporary freedom of driving down to the village for "café con leche" in a convoy of cars. It must have been quite a sight, but I wonder what message that gave to the boys back in the huts, digging their tunnels and planning their escape? If Steve McQueen had driven into the tarmac recreation area in that blue sweatshirt of his, revved his motorbike up loudly and driven up fast over the mound and escaped over the compound wall, I don't think I would have been surprised. There would have been a huge cheer from all of the inmates rattling their tin coffee mugs against the bars on their windows, and general confusion amongst the guards organising themselves to give chase to Steve.

"It'll be solitary confinement for you Steve if they catch you, and for one whole month mate. Better get that baseball ready to throw against the wall, like only you can."

Bounce, bounce, bounce … bounce, bounce, bounce.

I made my break about two months later. Looking back on it, I could probably have stayed there longer, and made the most of it, and yes I should have. In a perfect world. However, I was not very normal at that point, I had lots of ideas rattling around in my head and I was a pretty unhappy twenty three year-old. Being confined to my Persil-white infirmary each and every night on my own was probably not the best thing in the world for me at that time. However, my Spanish had definitely improved, as had my masturbation technique.

I caught the night train back from Malaga, up to Madrid, and went from there to Bilbao in the very North of Spain. Now that was like going from Spain into Switzerland in one very short journey, leaving the dusty heat of Andalucia for the lush green of Espana del Norte with its hills, its healthy valleys and rivers, its pine trees and Alpine-like houses, all very different from the land the tourist thinks of as "Espana." I then took a train across the French border, near to Perpignan where the year before I had got horribly drunk one night on red wine, (to start with), and had been crowned "Miss Tentrek 1982". Rory came runner-up, sorry mate, next time. Great legs though. "I would".

I think we must have arrived in Paris, and then travelled up to the Northern French Coast arriving at Dieppe very late one cold March evening. Now at this point, I should explain that I have always suffered from travel sickness. Always have since I was a young boy, that's of course if I ever stopped being that young boy. If you ever want to get a secret out of Nick, you only need to put him in a car or on a boat with no view at all of the horizon or the outside world, and you'll get me to tell what you need to know in under five minutes. Make that three. Fill the cabin with diesel fumes coming directly from the boat's engine, and that time falls to under two minutes, really! The train journey was okay, but I was now going to get on a cross-channel ferry from Dieppe to Newhaven that took over three hours on a perfectly calm day. Such was my enthusiasm to get back home that I had not really planned this key stage in the journey very well at all, not given my poor ability to travel well that is.

Remember this was March, and this was a very cold March evening, very cold indeed. As we stepped out of the cramped rusty green bus that had taken us from the train station to the ferry, it became clear that it was a windy evening too, actually very windy.

"So Nick, let's just take stock at this point, shall we? You have been travelling from the South of Spain to the North of France for the past thirty six hours, is that correct?"

"Yes, correct".

"You're tired, you're hungry, you need a shave and shower, and you have very little money left, would that be about right?"

"You got it".

"I hear you're not a great traveller. The train was fine, because you sat by the window all of the time that you could. However, you're now about to get onto a cross-channel ferry for at least three hours, maybe three and a half hours to go across the North Sea from France back to the south coast of England, and it's March. And you don't like boats do you? It's very cold, clearly very windy, starting to rain, and it's now dark too. Did I get that right?"

"Er, yes, that's about it ".

And so we boarded, the diesel fumes already had a heady perfume all of their own. There weren't many people on board, as you might imagine in March and we found a place where we could all quietly sit individually, read, eat or sleep. No iPods in those dark days I'm afraid. I was the nervous guy, hunched-up in the corner at the front of the boat, - is that the aft or poop, I never did know?! I was the British guy straining to see some kind of horizon through the now rain-soaked window, as we reversed out of Dieppe harbour that night.

Those three hours turned in to five and a half. "Heavy seas" the loud-speaker told us, "we can't unfortunately make the progress that we might have liked" and then we had to wait off the English coast while the weather abated enough for us to make our entrance safely into the harbour area. By the way, after just ten minutes, I simply had to leave the warmth and light of the boat's interior and go outside. I would not have lasted eleven minutes, really. And so, in order to avoid vomiting up my SNCF baguette de fromage from the last leg of the French train journey, I spent the cross-channel trip frozen to the handrail on the front left-hand side of our boat, desperately looking out into the March blackness for something that looked like a horizon, or even another vaguely stable boat that I could have fixed my gaze on in order not to be sick. A nice bright firmly-fixed oil rig would have been just the ticket, but it turned out that they haven't built too many of these in the busy shipping lanes of the English Channel and I so I never did locate one that night. Shame.

I don't think that I was even supposed to be out on the deck that night, I am sure that it was not safe. Looking back on it, no-one even knew that I was up there, but you see I had no choice. "The Mariner's cooked English breakfast served all day with fresh mushrooms at just £1.75" was pretty tempting, oh yes, but in the interest of my fellow passengers it was appropriate that I decline this oh so tempting offer.

Putting my feet firmly back on dry land was good that early morning. If you suffer like me from travel sickness, you'll know only too well that the draining nausea and the need to fully empty your stomach of recent contents do not go away actually for quite some time after you are on dry ground, not for several hours in fact. It had been a long night, a long cold and dark night, with no sign of fixed oil rigs, and my stomach muscles were well exercised as a result.

I got back home mid-morning. Claire I think was out at college and Dad was at work. I don't remember a great warm welcome from Dad that day, I can't even be sure that he was pleased that I had come back at all in fact. It all seemed very disappointing.

What was clear in a moment was that from now on things were changing.

A few nights later, Dad was having a shave and a bath one evening. He didn't normally have a shave in the evening, having had one already in the morning before going off to his surgery. I think I had brought him up a cup of tea into the lovely blue and yellow- flowered wallpaper that was our bathroom on the first floor in 16 Manor Way. It was special waterproof bathroom paper I'll have you know, good stuff in its day. Yellow and blue, with lots of small and medium-sized flowers on it, and waterproof, what more could you ask for?!

"Here's your tea Dad, okay?" (open and friendly)

"Thanks Nick" (pre-occupied)

"You going off somewhere tonight? (again, open and friendly)

"Yes, I'm taking someone out". (Cold, and factual, a little challenging)

You may have heard the joke that a Man's definition of Foreplay with his wife or girlfriend is asking her what her name is first? You can laugh now, Ha-Ha!! Well, that brief floral bathroom conversation was Dad's idea of preparing his son for the fact that he was starting to see someone else for the first time after Mum's death. At least, he certainly wanted me to think that it was his first time.

That was the sum of the imagination and flair that he could muster in order to introduce to me what I think you'll agree was a new idea and an important moment in our relationship, given what had happened in the spare room immediately directly above us on the second storey in November 1980.

Oh, how our Dad was changing. And not for the good. Oh no.

Some weeks later, we met his new friend Diana and we had lunch in our house. How nice our mother's watch looked on her wrist.

How confidently she walked about our home. How interesting her plans to change the house. Our house, not hers. But now more her house apparently.

This was followed some weeks later by a hugely awkward evening for the four of us at "The Gay Hussar" restaurant near Leicester Square in London. Not that Dad would have noticed, for his sight was beginning to change. Not his eyesight you understand, but what he chose to see with his eyes. My toes were curling.

There was nothing gay about that evening for Claire and I Dad. We were entering into a trap, Claire and I, and we didn't have the means, financial, emotional or otherwise, to stop and go back.

Trapped, by Dad. Our own Dad.

How our father was changing.

If ever you want to make an observation of a human being changing his/her behaviour, then take a look at Brian Holbrook in 1983.

I think he was already completely unrecognisable.

Some weeks later, we were at Woolwich Town Hall with Dad marrying this stranger. What a lovely day we had, just lovely. Wouldn't have missed that for the world Dad. I wasn't sure whether to run away or to follow Mum's lead, really. It was a grotesque experience for us Dad. Thanks so much.

Trapped, and by our Dad.

Dad had now forgotten about us completely. From now on, he had eyes and ears for one person only. I don't think he had any interest in us.

Brian Holbrook, you stopped loving your children in 1983, and you never loved them again. Fact.

I should have decked you and left you then forever. But I couldn't. I was trapped. I was financially dependent on you while I learned to teach at Sheffield University. That was vital to me so that I could stand on my own two feet.

Also, was I ever really going to end the relationship with the one parent that I had left ?

We needed you Dad then more than ever, we needed you to be our bedrock in our fragile lives. We had lots of good things in our lives but Claire and I had a driving need to have a base in life that we could go back to, whenever we needed to. You were required as our father to be there at that base whenever we needed to talk with you, and you had abandoned it. So, you abandoned us too didn't you Dad? Much easier than sticking around for your kids wasn't it?

Useless man. Weak man. Turns out you had no backbone.

And so, the destruction began. We were not allowed to talk about Mum.

There were no photos at all of Mum in the house.

There were no family photos of Brian, Audrey, Nick and Claire anywhere.

Dad cut me off in mid-sentence one day as I was talking about a family holiday that we had years before. Can't even remember the details, it was a genuine conversation that we must have been having about something. And then Diana walked into the room and Dad looked at me in a disapproving way and said

"Ssshh, be quiet now".

This was not Dad, not the Dad that I had loved and known for twenty years. Not the Dad who had loved me back. We were now living with a very different man, and more significantly a very changed man.

All of the past family experiences and holidays and friends, they were nothing apparently. I won't bore you with all of the details here, but believe me when I say that Dad allowed his new wife to say anything that she wanted to about our friends and our family life, and he let her say the most insulting and inaccurate things about people who mattered most to us, and he did nothing about it.

Nada, niente, rien. The stupid, dumb, bastard just stood by and let these things be said, and he watched as Claire and I were hurt to the core and he said nothing and he smiled.

And sometimes he even laughed.

What a fool you were Brian Holbrook, what a traitor to your children. How you hurt me.

Do you know what hurt me most of all Dad? It was your blatant disloyalty to your first wife Audrey Moss, our Mum.

I'm afraid that it was at this point that for me Dad, that you lost your integrity.

How I wish I had found the courage to look you in the eye and tell you that.

I'd have spat in your face too, if I had somewhere to run to afterwards.

Claire and I were clearly surplus to requirements. Put more simply, we were in the way.

Brian Holbrook, we no longer knew you. Neither did Audrey Robinson and she had known you for far longer.

Some of my most treasured possessions were just thrown away by Diana. School books, clothes, and the letters that Mum and I had written to each other when I was in Spain as a student in the summer of 1980, just months before Mum killed herself. I don't believe that I now have one single example of Mum's handwriting left. Mementoes, diaries, scrap books, holiday things, school and university books, all thrown away.

What a fucking useless father you turned out to be Brian Holbrook.

Just when we needed you most, you were furthest away.

I just wanted to put the record straight. I heard once that it's good to do that. People can perhaps then move on.

Fact is you failed us pal.

Big time.

Chapter 7 – Tapes that played

Quietly playing in the background

I finished reading a business book recently called "Crucial Conversations". It's good, very good. Go out and get it. You can probably guess by the book's title that it focuses on conversations and discussions that the authors, (there are rather unusually four of them), think are particularly important. The basic idea in the book is that at key times in our lives, and this can be in our working lives as well as in our personal relationships, there are conversations that need to be had because they are disproportionately important. In other words, the outcome of these conversations is much higher than that of others. These are not ordinary, day to day discussions, these are high-value ones. Things are at stake. There is something riding on this discussion that has an unusually high value, and so the conversation needs to be had and ideally planned so that it may take place successfully. Most crucially, the author points out that the conversation simply must take place and not be ignored or avoided. The biggest mistake might be that it doesn't happen at all, and if this is what happens, things will fester and no-one will be able to move forward. Are you with me so far?

Hence the title of their excellent book "Crucial Conversations".

Well, in the book the authors lay out an idea that one of the reasons that a relationship can become unhealthy or even worse go very badly wrong, is because things that need discussing openly and fully, do not get discussed like they need to be. They may get partially discussed, or in some cases the discussions that are just screaming out to be had, never actually take place, ever.

This may happen for any one of a number of reasons. One of the participants may not wish to have that conversation, or perhaps both are so entrenched in their positions that neither of them does. Maybe they need a third party to suggest that they get together and talk but there is no-one appropriate that can facilitate the meeting. And so, the dispute continues, it rumbles on, nothing gets discussed or resolved, bad feelings continue to grow, you get the picture.

Now, what happens in this kind of situation is that messages and ideas get heard over and over again. Often, this may just be in people's heads. We may repeat things many times over in our heads, things that have actually only been said or heard just once for instance. You can guess already, that this cerebral repetition then re-enforces the ideas and the possible prejudices that both sides have about each other and so the entrenchment gets even greater. An impasse is reached and a vicious circle is entered into.

The authors talk about "Tapes that get played" ie: things that we are told regularly, or which we hear in our heads over and over and over again. (I am not talking about actual cassette tapes here you understand). If we hear something enough times, it starts to take on an unshakeable truth of its own. Over time, it may become something so firmly fixed in your mind that you're not prepared to change your opinion on it, or to negotiate on it in any way whatsoever. Familiar = right. A compromise may be something that you can't even contemplate, after all it's "sacred".

This is what we mean by "tapes that play in your head".

Looking back on our family life in Manor Way, and I mean right back to when Claire and I were very young children, I am sure that there were several tapes that were played in our family and with some considerable frequency. Deliberately too maybe.

One good one for starters that Mum and Dad played was that Claire and I were adopted and that our being adopted "made you special".

"Your Mummy couldn't look after you but we wanted to look after you very much" was another.

16 Manor Way

"Being adopted makes you particularly special, and we are now your Mummy and Daddy".

You get the message I hope, for these were tapes that were played to us from very young I am sure. They are positive ones I think you would agree. I think Mum and Dad introduced the adoption idea to us very well when we were very young and they made a success of that together as far as I can see.

I think that there were other tapes that played in 16 Manor Way too, some perhaps not so good. I can't understand for example why Claire and I never asked Mum what had happened to her parents. I do not remember one single conversation as we grew up about our mother's upbringing, about her family life or her parents, not one. I found out long after Mum had died that her father had been alive while we were growing up as kids, and I would very much like to have at least known something about him, or to have seen some photos of him. Mum had fallen out with him after her own Mum died, we were told in another tape, and hadn't seen or spoken to him in many years I believe. I always knew that I was not biologically related to him in any way, but I would still have been naturally interested in knowing about our Mum's childhood, and her Mum and Dad, and where they lived, and what they did at weekends, and if they went on summer holidays, and so on. But that was a road that was shut off to us.

I don't recall these things ever being discussed even once. I am equally certain that two young children like Claire and I would have asked their Mum about her parents at some point in time. I think things must have been said when we were very young that had the effect of tapes being played in our heads. In other words, we probably grew up with a sub-conscious belief that we don't speak about Mum's parents because "they died long ago", or "Mummy fell out with them some time ago and has not seen them in years", or something like that. There was an idea planted in our heads I believe, probably from very early on in our lives, that we don't discuss this. The only thing I did know about Mum's childhood was that she had a doll of some kind called

"Tommy Brick", and that must have been very important to her because it made her laugh. These were the tapes that Claire and I heard as we grew up together, and they had the effect of leading us down certain paths of discussion and thought, and I would say very definitely not down others. I would say that they were used deliberately to steer us away from certain topics. Now, don't get me wrong, I'm sure that this happens in other families, but if I look back through time, some of the very biggest things in our family life were just never discussed. They were avoided, denied or at best stepped round. Whoops, mind the elephant.

She had a lovely smile. Mum that is, not Tommy Brick.

How very sad that after living with Mum for nineteen years, that the only two things I know about her childhood are that her Mum died when she was young, (I don't know how young, the tape didn't play that far), and that Tommy Brick was in her life.
What tapes must have been played that we never discussed more about her family, how very sad is that?

Dad, your comments …?

Mum had a brother, Jack. He was married to a lady called Rene and they lived at
56 Valley Road in Solihull West Midlands. We never went there, once only perhaps and briefly at that. Cup of tea, that sort of thing, a small cup too. Rene was a teacher and Jack an insurance inspector. We would see them perhaps once every year or so but I think their visits were not easy. I sensed even as a young boy that there was real unease between Mum and her brother Jack, and I think too with Dad and he. I seem to remember that they rarely stayed for more than a day or so, and not once did we see them over a Christmas period. Claire and I knew very little about them, or about Mum and Jack growing up together, or their parents, and I am very sure that tapes had been played from very early on in our childhood around all of this.

"Road ahead blocked, turn left you two if you wouldn't mind, please."

I wonder what stories there were, what secrets there were. The one tape that I do remember being played here was from Dad to the effect that "Mum's Mum died when she was very young and she didn't get on with her father's new wife".

Hhmm, just imagine that Dad, what a thought.

The last time that I saw Jack and Rene was at Mum's funeral in November 1980. When Sue and I got married in 1991, I remember Dad suggesting that I might want to invite them to our wedding, but the tone of his voice made it clear that he did not really want that to happen. Family unease indeed. What lay beneath the water I wonder.

So many questions and so few answers.

A similar secrecy shrouded Dad's family, particularly his father. Dad was born in 1928 and so the relationship that he had with his parents would have been very different to my relationship with him, and even more so when compared with the way that Jack and Sophie behave with Sue and I as their Mum and Dad today. I bet that I give our children more cuddles and hugs and have more laughs and jokes with them in a single month than we had with Mum and Dad in nineteen years. Literally. A generation thing, yes, but not totally so I think.

Dad graduated as a Medical student very early on, he was remarkably young so I was told by his fellow medical colleagues. His father died before Dad had graduated, which must have been distressing for our Dad. I think that Leonard Holbrook died of a kind of cancer, and that our Dad had been asked to give his opinion on his own father's illness as a studying medical student. I have long had the idea in my head that Dad gave an incorrect diagnosis and was particularly sad when his father passed away very suddenly. I can't tell you more than that, but that idea has been in my head for some years now from a brief and subdued discussion that I had with Dad just the once. There was probably a tape that played around that. I think that Dad and his sister Betty had fallen out about this at the time too. I think there was some distance between the two of them ever since. More than a northern formality methinks.

Now, our children will know all about my Mum and Dad and how they died, although I have not told them about Mum just yet. I think the idea of suicide would be hard to take at the age of ten, don't you? But when they ask, they will know all that they want to.

I am sure that in some ways, we all play tapes within our own families. That's to say, we may say the same thing about a particular subject or an individual on many occasions which leads to an idea or an impression becoming fixed in another person's head. Most of the time, it's not done deliberately, mainly through habit. However, I do believe that there was a key difference in the case of our family and that several tapes were played and that they were played with intent. I am not suggesting that there was a dark purpose or anything at all like that.

However, I am pretty certain that both of our parents had experienced some sadness in their lives and that they were both hopelessly poor at being open about this or confronting it.

I think this was something that had been set in stone in their personalities long before Claire and I came along and it was now wired into them as were being adopted. This is what I meant earlier in this book about something that happened to Mum around 1936, having great impact on my life so many years later.

The clearest example here was without doubt Mum's drinking, this should have been faced up to and treated in some way as a matter of great urgency many, many years ago. It wasn't. I reckon that Claire and I found ourselves with two parents who were masters at "sweeping things under the carpet". It got to be a rather large carpet too I'm afraid as there was a lot to sweep under it. Both were very good at tip-toeing round that large grey elephant in the corner there, you know the one that we can all see, smell, touch and hear and yet we never refer to.

"Dirty big grey one, over there, in the corner, the one with huge ears that you can't miss. Inside the living room with us, and yet somehow larger than the whole house, if you understand my meaning."

"Anything but talk about you know what. Oh no, we don't want to mention that, or him or her, do we now? Besides, that's all a long time ago now. No, that's passed", (and here comes one of Dad's ominously favourite phrases now), "we've drawn a line under that now. It's closed."

Yeah, right. Let's draw a line under Mum shall we? How very helpful that will be to us as your kids. And you were a medical professional Dad? Really? Where did you graduate from then, EuroDisney?

Yeah, right, that thing that you think is closed is actually a gaping wide sore in our lives that could not be more open.

You just can't face up to it, and we pay the price for that.

Here's an interesting footnote to this chapter. See if you can make some sense of this, I can not. About five months before Dad died in August 2005, I went down to Kent to see him for lunch, it was a Thursday. Our relationship had been hanging by a thread for many years by then, not that he would have known that. We had a very pleasant walk by the river where we used to fish, it was a warm afternoon. Not that you could tell from Dad's thick corduroy jacket and white woollen hiking and fishing socks that were best worn in the winter. He seemed to like wearing them all year round, even on the hottest of summer days. Bit of a Brian Holbrook trademark those thick, white socks, bless.

We walked down to the local pub in Chilham called The Woolpack. It's a pleasant enough Kentish pub, with a few bed and breakfast rooms across the lane and they do reasonable food, nothing special but it's fine. Very pink walls on the outside. It would have been about 12.30 pm, and Dad and I sat down at a table and looked at the menu. He was not a well man by now and that whole process of choosing where to sit, then sitting at the table, reading a menu, ordering drinks, and giving our food order to the friendly staff there was painfully slow, and a little awkward.

Dad did his usual thing of offering to put a credit card behind the bar, he was always very generous like that. More than I am Dad! I believe that I treated him to lunch on this occasion. Let it be remembered that Dad could be a completely generous man at just a moment's thought, and that was a fine trait Dad to have. You had it in platefuls. You could be so very kind, and were. You used to be the best, at one time.

His choice of food was not an easy thing to make due to his Parkinson's and almost anything that he chose would have been difficult to eat in a pub where people could see him struggling to cope.

My lovely Dad who had taken me fishing hundreds of times was now an elderly and ill man, completely unable to cut up his own food in a lovely Kentish pub, the county in which he had first taken young Nick fishing at the magical age of four, and the county where The Holbrooks had spent so many wonderful summer holidays in their Kentish cottage.

As we drank our orange juice and mineral water, the conversation was just strained, at best. It had been that way since 1983 Dad, your fault, entirely your fault. We said whatever we said to each other with a pained difficulty, but with the love still there, and as he struggled to eat his ploughman's or whatever it was that he had ordered he said this to me. I heard it loud and clear and I was not mistaken. I'll just say that again, I heard it loud and clear and I was not mistaken. Dad said this to me, holding tears back-

"I feel like I have been a total failure to you both". Read that to yourself again. Go on.

I looked at him, and said nothing. Now who was avoiding the truth Nick?

He had failed Claire and I for the last twenty two years, but not for the first twenty. They had been fabulous, and in so many ways.

I couldn't bring myself to say anything. I remember then looking away from him.

If you knew this Dad, why then had you allowed it to happen? I don't understand.

It was of course all too late now to undo any of it, way too late. The time to do that was on the other side of that line that you had been so keen to draw Dad. How sad.

Chapter 8 – My Hero dies

I never stopped loving you Dad. Never.

Sunday July 31st 2005.

We went down to see Dad around 2.40 pm this afternoon. Our friend Lyn Parry looked after Jack and Sophie, and their cousins too from Basingstoke Stephanie & Ross who were staying with us for the weekend. Sue and I drove round the M25 down to Kent, a journey that had become harder and harder for me over the years. Not because of the M25 itself you understand and its famous traffic congestion, but because of who was waiting for me at the end of it. At times, I had turned round at the very slightest excuse.

We got to the hospital and found Dad still asleep. He wouldn't really wake up even hearing my voice, so we stayed with him as he was sleeping. About ten minutes later, through the side-window of the ground-floor ward I could see Anne and John Wood arriving and when they came into the ward Sue and I said hello to them. It was so nice to see them both again, they had been fine friends to our family throughout my life.

Dad then began to wake up, probably on hearing Anne's voice. Thanks Dad! Anne and I spoke with Dad together and he woke up a lot more – eyes wide open, engaging with us, understanding what we were saying and smiling a lot. He saw Sue and John too and spoke with them both, I think he was very pleased to see us all. Sue said he really woke up when he saw me. Sue and I had given him a little water.

Sue, John and I went to get a cup of tea in the exotic "Spice of Life Restaurant" and left Dad and Anne to catch up. They were probably catching up on old times – Anne said they would talk about the kids and Manor Way, and Dad said something like "we were very lucky". I know that he remembered those days and that he meant what he said. At one point in that afternoon, he said to me quietly "I don't want to die here, I want to die at home". He knew his situation I'm quite sure.

John, Sue and I chatted in the café and John told us about the Wood family and what they were all doing, and about Matthew's Russian wife and beautiful five year old daughter. It was really good to hear that Matt was doing well. John said that Dad was in a poor state, but that no-one knew how he was going to get on. He knew the overall direction that he was heading in of course, being a good GP too.

Dad was so much more alert than he had been on the day before when I was with him. He had hardly woken up at all that day, at least when I was with him for over six hours. I had given him a shave, not a very good one, and made some light jokes while doing it. It was all rather sad, with his bitch of a wife looking on disapprovingly just feet away. The tension was unbearable. I wanted to hit her.

When we went back to the ward, Claire was there, she'd had a lift down there from a friend as her car was not working. She got there about 3.30 pm, she was very upset and probably quite shocked at seeing Dad how he was in bed. It was the first time that she had seen him for quite some time I think. Anne was still with Dad, and John kissed Claire when she came back in and we all started talking with Dad. He was most definitely the centre of attraction this particular afternoon.

Dad winked his right eye at Sue when she came back in – we both saw it and looked at each other – that was nice Dad. My Dad. The one I grew up with, the one that I loved so deeply.

Claire went off to the loo a few minutes later and then Anne and John went back home, they'd been there most days so far, which was very kind of them. They live about twenty five minutes away towards Dover.

So, it happened in this way that I was with Dad on my own holding his hand, I was standing by the window-side of his bed. He was pretty alert still and knew what was going on.

He was also very upset and he said to me

"We've had our ups and downs haven't we?"

I said "More ups than downs Dad "

and he told me how sad he was about lost time, I heard him say that last bit. I told him not to worry and that we were fine. We hadn't been fine of course for the second half of our lives together, but this was not the time to say things like that. I was that good.

He said that we had pulled through it ok, I think he was looking for reassurance here, and I said

"You know you gave us one down with Di don't you, one very big down?"

He knew... and he was acknowledging it as much as he was able to. Claire said that he had apologised to her some time back. This was the closest that he had for me, now that he was so close to the end of his life. But it was all too late. So much pain and so much hurt over two decades and I had to bite my lip. Again. Crucial conversations that should have happened over the years but which didn't. Now, here in a hospital ward, we were paying the high price.

I gave him a shave with just him, Claire and I there – did quite a reasonable job, from the locker-side of the bed. He seemed pleased that I had. We then talked about how he needed a haircut, and I asked him if he remembered Hext Hairdressing salon in Blackheath Village where Mum used to go. He sort of knew the name, but didn't really picture it. Claire did... near the Post Office wasn't it?

He started to get sleepy again.

He said

"I don't want to die before going home".

I think that he knew where he was and also why he was there.

The doctor came in with the nurse and reconnected his saline drip. He needed this to keep the fluids up in his body.

The nurse and I sat him up in the bed, and Sue and I chatted with for a few more minutes. Claire had to go and get her lift back at 4.30 pm. I'm sure they were both pleased that they had seen each other again. Sue said that Dad was very pleased to see Claire there.
So he should.

Once we had propped Dad up in his bed, we spoke for a few more minutes, and then let him sleep.

Wednesday, August 3 rd 2005

Today …. has been sad. Dad went into a nursing home. My Dad, he shouldn't be there, not Dad.

We left him at about half-past six. He was in a nice room of his own. He was wearing his own blue pyjamas, with a very discrete yellow spot in the fine pattern.

The staff seemed very friendly, Salome, the Manager and Leanne and her colleague the young nurses on duty. Both of them local Canterbury girls. They attended to him once he was settled in and he ate a reasonable meal. That was good.

You shouldn't be there, not you Dad. You're a Doctor, you know about these things, and how they work but it's not supposed to happen to you, only to your patients. Not to you Dad, not you.

You're intelligent, well-qualified, a respected Professional. People have always looked up to you, Dr Holbrook. Now I look down on you, but only because you're in a bed.

Seeing what's going on around you isn't as easy for you as it once was, is it? That wretched illness has taken away much of your ability to speak with us, the simple ability to just talk. I know that we do get some of what you say, but I also know that we finish your sentences for you. We shouldn't do that, I know… forgive us, forgive me.

I told you that I love you, and you said back to me

"The feeling's mutual".

That was a little formal Dad, but perhaps intentionally humorous too. Yes, I like that idea.

I'm rich. But so very sad.

Claire and I drove into Canterbury early in the afternoon, a city that we had spent so much summer holiday-time in as kids. Then in the 1970s we had been young, carefree and happy, now in that same city in Kent, where we had so many family holiday, we were watching our Dad slipping away.

We walked through the impressive city gates that had been there for hundreds of years.

"They'll see us all out, old Boy" is what Dad would have joked about their age. He was right I'm afraid, dead right, as they are many hundreds of years old. They will see me out too I'm certain. They knew how to build gates and walls in those days all right.

We found a nice little pasta bar, took a seat and ordered our meal. Claire was keen to order a cider, careful sister … We chatted for a while and probably got more close in those few minutes than we had done since Mum had died twenty five years ago. We talked about some things in particular that amazed me, and if you don't mind I'll keep them between Claire and I. I'm so glad that we had that conversation together, me with my mineral water.

The meal was pleasant enough and we paid the bill and melted back into the touristic flow that is so often Canterbury. We were carried along towards the cathedral together with the other international strollers, and our multi-coloured group stopped outside the ancient cathedral gates to look up at the grey statues and gargoyles that have looked down on so many people over so many years from so many countries of origin. At one point, people would have come there on foot or on horseback, now they arrive on Airbus A319s and cross-channel ferries and rented convertible cars. Don't suppose the gargoyles mind that much, they certainly didn't look like they do.

Chiselled.

Fixed.

Time-less.

The cathedral was shortly closing and we had just enough time to go into the grounds and wonder around before they closed for the day. There was a kind of peace about the yard, the busy heat of the day was now passed, gone were the large groups of tourists and the final administrative tasks of the day were being completed. It felt special to get the opportunity just to be here at that time of the warm early evening, and Claire and I walked about the cathedral area casually. I'm sure that each of us was in our own thoughts. We said a few brief things to each other, neither of us practising Christians.

We found the cloisters and walked into them and then along them together. It reminded me so very much of walking the cloisters at school. We had a service in Westminster Abbey each morning and we left the confines of Westminster School and Little Dean's Yard to hurry along the cloisters to reach the abbey in time for the service. We just called it "Abbey". If a member of staff wanted to talk with you, he might say "Holbrook, come and see me in my study after Abbey".

Same natural light, same peace, similar history.

I said to Claire that I remembered her doing some super (a Dad word) brass-rubbings when she was at Blackheath High School, probably from the local church, and she told me a little about some of the challenges of brass-rubbing. "Not too light in your touch, not too heavy" she had said to me. I think she quite liked that walk with me.

She told me about the time that she had gone to see Dad for some medical advice not long after he had married and how his monstrous wife had told Claire that now she needed to go and find a regular Doctor as he was married to her and that she should not bother him any more about these kind of things.

You always were sheer poison Diana.

If only you had told me about this at the time Claire, I just might have sorted things out with Dad for once and for all, but I had no idea Darling. If only you had told me. I didn't know. Your failure Dad, again, to be there for your children.

We walked around the final quarter of the cloister and out towards the open yard again. There were some people coming out of the side door of the towering cathedral and I asked Claire if she wanted to slip in and see the cathedral inside.
She said no and that she would wait outside for me. I casually walked down the path, trying to look like someone who had just come out of the cathedral, whatever he would look like. Anyway, it worked and I moved inside the marbled hush that is Canterbury Cathedral, as people filed past me from whatever event they had been attending.

His purple gown first caught my attention as he stood talking with someone. I thought that I would linger for a few moments, in case I got the chance to say hello and ask if I might light a candle for Dad. His conversation ended and I reached out my hand to introduce myself to the Archbishop.

"Good evening sir. My father is in a nursing home just a few miles up the road from here, and he's dying for sure. May I light a candle for him?"

"Yes, of course. You must be very upset".

"I am sir you see we were once such great friends".

"May I ask how old he is, and what his name is?"

"My father's name is Brian Sir, and he is seventy seven and he has Parkinsons very badly. My sister and I are here together this evening".

"Please go ahead and light a candle for him, and I will be sure to say a prayer tonight for Brian. God Bless".

I was in tears throughout this brief conversation, and felt so weak. I lit the candle for you Dad, and by the way, the Archbishop was going to say a prayer for you later that night. I'm sure he would have too. That would have brought a smile to you I think. It brings tears to my eyes now as I remember it.

When I came back out into the reassuring warmth of the evening light, I walked up to Claire who was sitting on a metal bench to my right and I told her who I had just spoken with.

"Oh, good" came the reply. Consistent Claire, not impressed even in the slightest. Perhaps she had some deeper thoughts.

We wandered into the cathedral tourist shop but nothing really caught our eye, I'm sure that our thoughts were with Dad. It was strange to me that Canterbury, which had been a place of such great childhood family happiness in the 1970s in particular, was now a place where we felt such sadness as Dad neared the end of his life.

The Cathedral shop was closing, but the shop would open up again the next day, and on time.

But not Dad. His was about to close for the final time.

I couldn't write prose for Dad's funeral, it seemed empty. I did try, really, but the words didn't come naturally. It all seemed the wrong way to go about it.

This is what I wrote instead, and did I deliver it well for you and I Dad? I hope you could hear every word of it. I think he would have been especially impressed with this, wouldn't you "Old Boy"?

Claire wasn't at Dad's funeral. And that was okay Claire, really. I understand.

Semper Pater Meus

Hear some thoughts about my Dad,
Once the best I could ever have had,
A caring, listening man, and kind,
Of clearly intellectual mind

I'd like to think I knew him well,
But with friends and family who can tell?,
Familiar, and always around,
But is our understanding sound?

Victoria Avenue, No 30,
Schoolboy shorts, knees all dirty,
Lymn Grammar School, then Worksop College,
The start of all his copious knowledge

Smiling & laughing, "Dr H", they'd call,
Their friendly GP, familiarly bald,
Trained in London, up at Bart's,
Capturing a certain nurse's heart

A conscientious, committed doctor,
Your loyal receptionist Rene Proctor,
121 your "Palace of Healing",
Down in Greenwich, not in Ealing

Leave by eight, and you won't be late!
But nearer to nine, and there just isn't time.
Get up earlier Dad you really should,
Take a lead from young John Wood!

Caring for several thousand patients,
A career that surely needed patience,
Calling on your healing powers,
As a kid I remember you working long hours

I'd like to think I knew him well,
But with friends and family who can tell?

Familiar, and always around,
But is our understanding sound?

I think of you eating toast and curd,
Usually lemon, delicious I've heard,
And Patum Pepperium, or Gentlemen's Relish,
M & S Custard Tarts, how those you'd relish!!

I'll always remember, I'll never forget,
The custardy tart, yellow and wet,
For there slightly hidden, look there underneath,
Was a very good imprint of Brian Holbrook's teeth!

You'd click the spoon on the roof of your mouth,
As your Alpen with Orange Juice headed south,
And with sandwiches I could have bet one pound,
That you'd say to me "Well, perhaps, just one round"

In the sitting room in Manor Way,
Classical music you would play,
Usually after you'd had a light lunch,
A favourite pastime I have a hunch.

Relaxing in your brown chair's arms,
Blissful Rachmaninov and Brahms,
Carried along by Sir Edward Elgar,
Your English composer without a par!

I'd like to think I knew him well,
But with friends and family who can tell?
Familiar, and always around,
But is our understanding sound?

You told me once that you'd gone too far,
On money spent on motor cars,
Zephyr, Herald, Mercedes Benz,
Rather good for impressing friends…

NAN 692D,

16 Manor Way

KUV 949P,
TGU 74R,
Yours, then mine, our special car

On Saturday with your work all done,
We'd leave for Kent, somewhere around one,
Family hassle, and in a hurry,
Off we'd go to Canterbury

Cottages April, Rose, and Ivy too,
I simply can't make all their names rhyme,
But what we had was just sublime,
A golden, smiling, so happy time

I'd like to think I knew him well,
But with friends and family who can tell?
Familiar, and always around,
But is our understanding sound?

The Woods, the Hollicks, and Betty too,
A noisy but harmonious crew,
And with Robinsons we were the complete crowd,
A time of which I know you're proud.

You & Mum gave us many good things Dad,
A "triffic" educayshun's what we've 'ad,
You taught us to be open and true,
And if that is in us, then it came from you

The gift that you brilliantly gave to me,
And you really might have charged a fee,
The gift you gave has made me rich,
For it was you who first taught me to fish.

Oh there's golf, and then tennis, and they're quite fine,
A perfectly healthy use of time,
There's hockey and rugby if you dare,
But with fishing they simply don't compare.

Nicholas Holbrook

How you loved to get away,
"Gone Fishing" is what we say,
The challenge for you to catch him out,
That wary, cautious, wild brown trout

I'd like to think I knew him well,
But with friends and family who can tell?
Familiar, and always around,
But is our understanding sound?

You and I had fences to mend,
And we did that a little towards the end,
You spoke with me, and I with you,
And I do hope that what you said was true

There was a time so clean and pure,
What could make that not endure?
Those years we had, our time together,
Dad, why didn't that last forever?

Dark clouds were forming in our sky,
Should have stopped them you and I,
How crucial it was that we should try,
Should have stopped them you and I

I can't sum up all your life Dad,
For me to try that would just be mad,
Much will be said today by others,
Betty Hitchcock said you were "like a brother".

I can't sum up all your life Dad,
Nor the Ups & Downs that Brian & Nick had,
But I do hope that I knew you well,
But with friends and family who can tell?

We'll meet again, on that lake in the sky,
You'll have gone fishing, and so will I ….
These my thoughts about my Dad,
Once the best I could ever have had.

And so, the man who was for so long my hero had now slipped away.

Bye Dad.

I think of you every hour of every single day. I miss you in my life hugely.

I think you might know that.

Chapter 9 – Dad's Will – No-one can believe it

Another little challenge

You don't know this as you read this story, but this chapter was written out of sequence. Let me explain. For the record, I am writing this on a Friday evening, the 9th September 2005 in fact. I won't forget today in a long, long time, and I don't think a lot of people associated with The Holbrook family will either.

I don't have a relationship with my father's second wife Diana. She could drop to the floor now with a heart attack and my only concern would be for the floor and that it was a long-drawn out process. I loathe this person, really.

I don't have those feelings for anyone else and I never have before. I understand that it's not normal, but then neither is what we've had to go through with her normal.

My father died just over three weeks ago. It has definitely not sunk in at all, not even slightly, not even to the tune of just one percent that my Dad will no longer be around in my life. Can't believe it…

Since we have no relationship with his second wife, Sue my wife wrote to her (Diana) to ask if we could get some family property such as personal papers, jewellery, photos and so on. A letter came back today in which we learned that my father's second wife had been made "Sole Beneficiary" of his will.

I don't think I knew how to respond. Angry, resentful, now just plain tired of it all. Above all, I found myself in complete disbelief and shock. Complete, almost unable to move. I still am six hours later, no more taking it in now than I did earlier this afternoon when Sue told me first.

16 Manor Way

Dad, if you're up there listening, what in hell's name have you done? I know you were ill, but what have you let happen? After all that we've gone through as a family, we now find out that Claire and I, your daughter and son, have knowingly been cut out of your will. "Sole beneficiary" when we know what you wanted, after you had told us what your wishes were, and in front of Sue… just not fair.

A total injustice, not what we and several close friends know for a fact that you wanted. Not what you wanted, not what you wanted to happen, not what you wanted to put us through as we grapple with what we need to grapple with – adoption, alcoholism, suicide, family breakdown, your death three weeks ago, ….and now this.

You've been "had" Dad, your final wishes have been polluted. They were changed, probably about six months ago by your poisonous wife, and now you're gone, we have the taste of her in our mouths.

Thanks pal.

I feel gutted. I feel betrayed, - again. I feel sorry for Claire most of all, as she needs a cushion to support her as she goes through her world in her own struggling way.

Sue says I shouldn't be cross with you Dad, is that right? Sue says I should be cross with your hateful wife, not you. You were likely asked to change your will as you were suffering so noticeably from dementia. I guess you just rolled over and agreed – said "yes", accorded, fitted in, complied, took the easiest route, did as you were asked, signed on that dotted line – "Oh, look, here's a pen I got you".

Was that how it happened Dad, was it? WAS IT? WAS IT? I could call you a bastard tonight for letting this happen. And who's to say that I'm wrong?

Your children have been cut out of your will. That's not right, it's not that thing we call "fair" that we hold so dear in our lives, and it was not what you wanted. Because you told us what your wishes were that day in Kent, and they weren't this were they?

Our Mum's jewellery, the stuffed fish in that wonderful Cooper bow-fronted glass-case, your Mark IV Carp Fishing rod, family photos probably, personal papers, things I probably don't even know about, … and we can't get to them, at them, near them, around them, to see them, touch them, feel them, re-connect with them, to take them back, to re-member them.

We can't do it, not legally.

We'll contest it Dad, for what we once had, for what we once had in The Holbrook Family…tonight, I feel like I've been punched in the face. We all do.

I don't believe that I will sleep well tonight Dad. I hope you do….?

16 Manor Way

A letter to Anne Wood -

1.55 am, Wednesday 14th September.

Dear Anne,

You can see the time at which I'm writing this letter to you. You and I spoke last night, thank you so much for taking my call and listening to me. If I can't pick up the phone from time to time to speak to Anne Wood, Audrey Robinson or either of the Betties, then we've really had everything taken from us.

You can not begin to know what Claire and I are going through at the moment.

Apparently, Dad's will dated October 2003 passes everything to Diana – fullstop. She is the only beneficiary. Nothing goes to anyone else at all, now or ever in the future. This news has crushed both Claire and I, and Claire has taken it particulary badly. I thought our days of crying were long over, but apparently not.

I've known Diana Rowley since sometime in 1983. They're not fond memories. I've a good idea that she and Dad knew each other before Mum took her life. I can't prove that. Strangely enough, I never challenged Dad on that, such was the deep love between us that I just didn't. I probably should, I know that whatever he told me would have been the truth.

Diana over those years has inflicted colossal damage on Claire and I, and was the cause for huge damage to be done to our relationship with our Dad in particular. Anne, it was like he had been physically drugged – whenever there was an issue of any kind, he would simply take Diana's side and completely back down from supporting his children. It was like we were total strangers to him, - us!!

Seven years ago, she told Sue that Mum was a lesbian. Can you believe that? I told Betty Hitchcock that too by the way, you can imagine her reaction. At Claire's wedding to Graham, when she saw Audrey Rob and Sally there to take pictures (which was entirely normal and loving that Audrey was there), she said "What's that woman doing here?" I could go on and on and on and on and on, with comments and horrible things said throughout the years, you get the picture.

None of the Manor Way crowd had or have any idea of this. All they see is Diana looking after Dad in his illness. That bit was true, but it doesn't show the whole picture. <u>Please do let John read this letter too.</u> I think he thinks that Diana is probably a wonderful person – John she so is not. Something in her causes her to be unbelievably horrible, and we've been in the line of fire for twenty years plus.

I believe that in October 2003 Diana persuaded Dad to change his will in some way. I know that Dad's health was already poor at that stage – that's not a guess, it is based on accurate memory of specific meetings and lunches with him. You will probably know what state he was in then too. Furthermore, I believe that his revised will did not reflect his wishes as he had told them to Sue and I, <u>with Diana present at the time</u>. Claire also knows what Dad had told her, as does Betty Hitchcock from her lunch with Dad in September of last year 2004. I also believe that Betty Walker knew what Dad's wishes were. This revised will was not what Brian Holbrook wanted with regard to his children – I am certain that he was put under very considerable pressure by Diana to change it.

Think of how he must have felt about that, if he knew what was going on ….
So, Anne, I would like to think that all of the lovely comments that you made to me on the phone last night were true. It sounded like Mum meant a lot to you. I do hope they were, at the moment, I'm not sure of anything. I don't know who to trust, and who's telling me the truth.

I want to apologise for something to you in this letter too which you don't even know about. When I first called you about Dad's will last week, I perhaps did not explain the implications very clearly. You didn't know from our conversation that Diana was the sole beneficiary did you, and what that means? When I told this to you on the phone, you switched subjects very quickly to tell me that you had taken up fishing recently. When I put the receiver down, my cynical mind then started to suggest to me that you and John might have been present in some way when Dad's will was changed, and that John as the outstanding Medical Professional that he is, might have been a witness to Dad's revised will, saying that Dad was of sound mind. If this was not the case, then I do apologise to both you and John. You can see that we don't really know who even believes us at the moment. Actually, I know that Audrey's understanding of all of this is very accurate, and Betty's too, and I'm sure that you are a good loyal friend to Mum and Dad. Forgive me for saying all of this will you? Mat would probably have something to say on this too to me for even thinking it. It's an indication of the damage that had been done that I even began to think in this way about you.

Anne, I'll wrap up my letter here, and thank you for reading this. Thank John too will you?
I think I'll pop a copy of this in the post to Audrey and Betty too, I know that they both want to know what's going on. I called her yesterday evening. Betty and Dick are more shocked at this recent news than I had first realised.

Finally just to re-cap for your benefit, in Dad's house there are Mum's items of jewellery, Dad's Mum's items too, Dad's father's pocket gold Hunter watches, Claire's Christening bracelet, letters from Mum to Dad from when they were first going out, Holbrook family photo albums, and old Holbrook cine films from the 60s and 70s. Diana is denying that any of these exist and will not return them to us. I would not be surprised if they have all been thrown out, literally. What kind of person would behave in that way? How and why would they be so jealous of The Holbrooks?

Love to you and John for all of your friendship over so many years Anne. Write back to me if you want to, I keep all of Audrey's letters.

Nick –

No reply ever came back to me.

I wonder who I can trust?

I wonder what relationships really lasted from the past and which matter now?

Another of Brian Holbrook's legacies.

Too, too late. It's now all just too late.

Chapter 10 - Claire

Just not right

I have an iPod, and mine is pink. It's one of the very early ones, it's a 2 megabyte iPod Mini, finished in metallic pink actually. Not as light as the models that followed, but particularly cool I think, it's bit of a classic. Think I'll have it for many years actually, rather like my Audi A6. Good design never fades…

This particular evening, it was a bright and dry April evening at about 6.50 pm, and I was going for a run. With my particularly cool, metallic pink iPod you understand. It's bound to help me run faster, all that good running music to speed me along.

I was just strapping the iPod onto my left arm and getting the earpieces ready to go into my ears, when the phone rang.

"Jack Darling, could you get that for me please?" I called out.

"Sure Dad" replied Jack, he was rather good at answering the phone. Not quite as good I have to say as his younger sister Sophie but he can do it pretty well. On went my iPod, strapped securely to my upper left arm, and now it was just time to put the earpieces in so that they wouldn't fall out as I jogged along.

"Dad it's Graham, for you" said Jack.

"Oh, thanks Matey, I'll just have a quick chat with him and then head off for my run". I took the phone from Jack the secretary to talk to my brother-in-law.

"Hi Graham, how are you?!

"Not great, mate. I have bad news"

"Why, what's happened?"

"It's Claire, she's been found dead in her flat".

A few moments …

"What happened Graham?" I immediately thought that she had taken her own life.

Struggling through tears and shock, Graham explained to me that he had been driving through Steyning in Sussex with their children in the car, when he noticed police cars outside Claire's flat. Graham and Claire had been separated and then divorced at this point probably for about two years.

He could see it was not going to be good with so many police cars there and he instantly felt that it was going to be bad news, bad news about Claire. Remember that Graham had Russell and young Katy their children in the car with him.

I don't know all of the details but he must have parked the car nearby, gone over and spoken to one of the police officers, and been told.
Claire had not been seen for several days, about four, possibly five I think. Her friends locally had arranged to have a drink with her one night and had knocked on the door to get her, but there had been no reply. One of them had put a note through the door to say that they had called, "See you down the pub", that sort of thing. I know because I found the note on the floor a few days later, written on a pub meal receipt. The note would have landed on the doormat, just ten feet or so from where Claire already lay.

Claire had been working as a secretary at the Sussex Police offices, on the South Coast, and her work colleagues thought it strange that she had not called in sick or left some kind of message.

She had a difficult Manager there that she worked for so she might have been excused taking a day off to get away from what was becoming an unpleasant situation. Claire told me that several other girls there did not like working with this Supervisor. However, Claire was not pretending to be sick or anything like that, for there was another reason that she had not been seen over that weekend, another reason why she had not returned people's calls or numerous text messages.

Claire had died quite suddenly of Meningitis. We understood that it was extremely rare for an adult to die of this illness, extremely rare. Another two months, and she'd have had her forty fourth birthday in June. A great time of year to have a birthday Claire.

Several people thought that Claire might have taken her own life, I was one of them at first. I guess that this way of passing on was perhaps better. Bud Robinson told me that she would have died quickly, and probably slipped into unconsciousness first. I hope so.

I think that she had been dead for three days when her body was found.

I expected to outlive my parents. That was likely to be the case. But not to outlive Claire.

I walked into the chapel where Claire's body was laying in her coffin. How final was it to see that?

Still, wooden and silent. Not Claire, her coffin.

Somehow I thought I could feel the weight of the coffin and her body even though I had not touched it or carried it in any way at all. I wonder how the mind works that it can sense weight just through sight alone? Just a perception I guess. Like imagining that you are rooted to the ground like an English oak tree so that no-one can pick you up. Ever tried that one? Amazing how it works isn't it? You imagine that your legs carry on down deep into the ground just like tree roots, and hey-presto, the guy that tries to pick you up, the very same guy that did that so easily just one minute ago, simply can't.

I so wanted to see her face and kiss her goodbye, but that was not possible. The autopsy you see ... The last time that I had seen Claire was at an Angel workshop in Wiltshire a little under three months earlier with some kind and good people attending. Thankyou Sarah.

I wrote this for dear Claire ... and I believe that I read it out at her funeral service. There were so many people there.

Many of them had not seen her for some years, but they still all came Claire because they wanted to. More people than will ever come to mine.

16 Manor Way

Claire

Claire's been taken from you and me,
At the confusing age of 43,
They say she's moved to a better land,
But this is something I can't understand

Some think she's gone to a place called Heaven,
What of her children, 15 and 11?
She left so fast, we'd much to say,
She thought we would talk another day

She seemed sad here, a troubled soul,
A sort of living but so not whole,
Out of place, and out of time,
Extracted from us in her prime

Chakras, Energies and Angels too,
Her journeying on to something new,
She touched us all, in her own way,
If I had faith, for Claire I'd pray

Claire had a raw deal in life.

Think about it for a moment.

She was adopted in circumstances that I don't know very clearly some time in 1962. Her natural family had a record of alcoholism, depression and suicide. She was adopted by a couple where the Mum was an alcoholic, had suffered from depression and then committed suicide. Just how bloody unfair was that on Claire, huh? Just what are the chances of that happening to her? Not just one out of the three things being thrust onto her, or two, but all three!

She really went into life with a heavy weight dragging behind her, and she never got to shake it off. If anything, it was added to.

Betty Hitchcock said that she thought that Mum never loved Claire. I think she meant that Mum had loved the first girl, also called Claire, but that when she was taken back by her natural mother, that Mum never really started to love our Claire, Claire No. 2 if you like.

Wow, how sad does that make me feel, to think that Mum may never have loved Claire. And Betty would know, she would probably be right. What chance did Claire have in her life then really? I don't mean the very obvious one about education and the neighbourhood where she grew up and where she went on holiday, but the deeper things inside you as a person, those things that make you who you are, which shape how you are, and which determine how you behave in this life.

Claire, Mandy as your Mum called you first, you had a raw deal. No doubt about it.

Chapter 11 – Making Sense of All of This

Sunday morning …

What was I put on this earth to do?
This I can't answer, tell me can you?

The pattern of habit, the daily grind,
When a reason or purpose is what I can't find

Oh don't get me wrong, there's good and there's bad,
I hope that I'm grateful for the good things I've had,

It's just that I really can't get around
To thinking that's why I was put on this ground

It's just not enough, I clearly need more,
It's a feeling I have right down to my core,

A yearning inside to develop and grow,
To use all my skills that I know I can show

I'm stuck in a rut, I'm trapped in some hut,
I'm trapped in my hut, and stuck in my rut.

It might well come, that moment in time,
When I learn in an instant that purpose of mine,

I know that it could, but not that it should,
It's something to drive, to make come alive,

I need to take action, to do something bold,
To make my mark clearly, as I nearer to old,

There will come a time when it's no longer me,
Someone else's brief turn, then they too will be free.

Maybe I won't get out of my bed,
Or ever nourish those ideas in my head,

Maybe that's my role, the reason I'm here,
To live my whole life enveloped in fear

Yes, maybe that's it, maybe that's it,
To be seen on this earth but not do my bit,

My reason for being here, I may never find,
As I drudge through routine, and the bland daily grind.

Questions, so many questions …but answers so few.

So what do I know now, after all of this? What is certain to me? What am I allowed to take away from 16 Manor Way, and what went on there?

For starters, I don't know why Mum took her own life. I don't think I ever will now. Not unless someone on their death bed writes to me or calls me and reveals something new to me that they want to pass on, before they too pass on. I have no reason to think that this is going to happen. What I do know is that I think about her every day, and often look at her photos, not that I have many of her. There's one here in my office, taken on a summer's day by a magical stream down in Kent in the 1960s. I remember it well. Mum is looking towards the camera, looking like there's something she knows, perhaps a sad thing, but trying to smile anyway. It's a slightly pained expression that I think I see on her face. Click went Dad's shutter, capturing the moment that I look back on now forty years later. At the time, on that sunny afternoon, it was just a photo that was being taken. Now, many years later, time attaches more significance to it and possible interpretations of Mum's facial expression come rushing to my mind.

I wonder what was in Dad's mind as he depressed the Pentax button.

16 Manor Way

You can see me just in the bottom right hand corner of the same photo, I'm about eight or nine, playing close by on the edge of the shallow stream. I'd love Mum to have met with Sue my wife, on one of her good days, one of her good, sober and happy days.

I think they'd have had a lot to talk about don't you, over tea? I wonder if Sue would have unlocked Mum's past. Dad didn't.

I know that Audrey wasn't my Mum, but you see Audrey was most definitely my Mum. How I'd love to go back in time and talk, and talk and talk with her again, endlessly. You see our relationship ended so very suddenly on that cold November night in 1980.

Audrey Hepburn, Audrey Holbrook. Mum.

Dad you know about. Nineteen years of family life together with him, always deeply impacted on by Mum's drinking, probably right from the first day of our adoption, but lots of good normal family stuff going on too, I hope. Then the meteors came, and they hit suddenly. And he destroyed all of that, for some reason that I will never, never understand. No more than I understand Mum's death.

He was a changed man. If you were a game of Premiership football Dad, you're absolutely screaming out to be described as "a game of two halves". What a contrast.
More significantly, what a great tragedy it was for you and me Dad, for Nick and Brian. For us. Not for the planet, or for mankind, but for two people who had a brilliant relationship that you opted to simply discard. Like a Starbucks plastic coffee cup. Not me. I fucking stayed with you right to the end. I was the last person from our family to be with you before you died in the Nursing Home. I never let rip with you even on the warm August evening when you slipped away from us finally.
Then Claire, so sad. Her passing on I can least accept. It really has not sunk into me over three years later. I want her to receive this book from my hand. I still have her Sussex telephone number written in my diary, I can't rub it out or cross it out or

even put a bracket round it. And so it stays. Maybe one day I'll call it just to see.

I like to think that she is still with us, but that she is also somewhere that she longed to be, away from this dull, material existence.

Flying with the other Angels.
And what of me, Nick? Arguably it's been the hardest for me as I have seen all of my first family die. They all had their issues and challenges, did Mum, Dad and Claire, but being the last one alive of the four has given me demons of my own to wrestle with. Many of these demons simply come from issues not being confronted over the years like they should have been, and from conversations that needed to be had, just not being had – truly crucial conversations.

Fundamental discussions that we ought to have had.

I am forty eight years young, happily married to Sue, and we have two wonderful children. Sue is the best thing that could ever have happened to me. But this is not a book about them and the future. It was written as a record of my past, our past, Claire's and Nick's, two children who were so fortunate to be adopted into an affluent middle-class medical family, but which was not quite as it seemed to the outside.

I feel like I am the only one that has any idea of the thoughts that drive so continuously round my head. I am sure that I must be. After all, who else is there to know them? Our family seemed so normal to everyone outside it, why would anyone even think that I still had any issues at all? They're all getting on with their lives, and their family stuff. No-one has ever said to me "Nick, you must miss Claire?" or "Do you think of your Mum on Mother's day or on January 20th, her birthday?"

These words don't come my way. I think them myself though.

"Surely, this was all in the past Nick, behind you, in the rear view mirror? Leave it, leave it alone. Drop it. Draw a line underneath it. Move on. Forget the past. It's gone, you can't undo it. Close the chapter. Look forward, look to the future. That was then, this is now. Never know what's round the corner. Bless."

"No, Nick's all right, no issues there … not in his head. He seems fine, recovered now that's clear to see. Yup, all okay with that one. I expect that he's forgotten most of that sad family stuff by now. All happened a long time ago you see, he'll have moved on I'm sure. After all, he doesn't look sad does he? Sorted."

Is it? How sorted?

Clowns do generally have a smile on their face you know. Hello.

Sue doesn't understand it, but she's about right when she says "Nick Holbrook, you're going through your own living Hell". I am in a way, and it's effected me so much. You see, here's how I am, married, at forty eight. This is me, Nick, after all of this that I have tried to put down on paper. I am all of these …

Lonely, loner, saddened.

I have no sense of belonging, no sense of origin, no sense of purpose. I have not even the slightest iota of belief that I am here for a reason. I am an accident, probably made out of Middle-England passion, but still an accident nevertheless.

I have no philosophy about human life that could be described as valuable. None that's worth writing down anyway. "Carpe Diem" is about as near as I can get, - you know "Make hay while the sun shines", "Make the most of it", "Take what you can whilst it's there", but then that notion too falls away within seconds doesn't it? Life can't be just that simple can it now? I don't think so. Oh, hold on, there goes an idea beginning to firm up, just for a brief moment.

Pessimistic, bitter, very angry.

There are things that I should have done. Lots of things. Here's the first. I should have put my Dad up against a wall and had one almighty, thunderous row with him the day before he got re-married and told him who he had become and what we was doing to Claire and I, what he was throwing away, shown him the poison that he was allowing into our family, the raw damage that he was doing, the things that he just didn't see, or was choosing not to see, the unbelievably naïve and crap judgement that he was showing almost daily, the pure destruction that he was causing around him, and I should have forced him to see him how much sheer hurt he was inflicting on those around him that needed him so very much. I should probably have pushed him to the ground and not let him get up until he was changed back to the Dad that we had known, until he had put right all of the ills that had crept into our family, like a good Doctor can, righted all of the wrongs, until he had made unsaid all of the horrid, horrid comments that his hideous second wife had said about all of us, until he had laid out clear ground rules going forward about our family that we used to have and how legitimate it was to talk and refer to that family whenever we fucking wanted to.

But I didn't. I should have, we all should have, but we didn't.

Should. Should. Should.

I even imagine where and when that conversation would have taken place, the two us out walking in a field in ambivalent Kent. How different things might have been if we only had.

Resentful, confused, probably depressed too.

I don't mix well. Put me in a large gathering, and I feel like I want to get out, and fast.

Make that a family gathering, with someone else's happy family around them, all having a good time, and the need to leave gets even more powerful. Almost overwhelming.

The need to run. My need is to escape.

All very simple to analyze I'm quite sure, because it's the pain of seeing around you what we too once had but no longer do, that becomes so unbearable. Can you see that Sue? Can you begin to see, just a little, why I find Christmas so hard? Or birthday celebrations, or large Sunday family gatherings? Implanted into someone else's family situation, I feel totally trapped. It puts my first family into context, it holds up a measure to The Holbrooks of 16 Manor Way and shows that we fell way short of the norm.

More than that, the older I get, the less I feel compelled to show even the most basic manners that I know are expected of us all, and stay around making polite conversation. This is not good I do know, but that's how I am. I've fucking done that for twenty years, pretending, and supporting Dad publically. That's how adoption and suicide and alcoholism has impacted on me, that's me now, that's Nick Holbrook, fifteen stone, and aged forty eight.

Anti-social, withdrawn, not normal.

So, here's how it worked in my case …. you could almost come up with an equation:

Adoption + Alcoholism + Suicide = one pretty uncertain guy. Even now.

I think that Claire was even further along on the scale than I am. Towards the top of the scale in fact. Bloody shame.

I don't believe that I really considered taking my own life. I think I thought I did, when I was in my mid-twenties, when I was so, so fucking miserable. Miserable and very confused. Nice one Father. Great job. Appreciate you looking out for us.

But I don't think I ever did come near to it. Perhaps I lived next door to it as it were, one step way eh? What I do know is that I would never have wanted anyone that I know to feel as wretched as I did as a twenty-six year-old. Those were truly deeply unhappy days, around 1986/1987 specifically.

Thank Heavens for my work then as a school Teacher. I enjoyed it very much, it kept me sane. It kept me alive.

Claire probably had deeper feelings, I don't know. What I do know is that I so wish that I had been there for her. Like the time that she called Dad up for some medical advice and his bitch of a new wife told her to go away and call someone else for medical advice now that he was re-married. This makes my blood boil as I am writing this. Should have been there with you Claire, to support you and stand up for you.

And then I'd have hit him too.

Less hard.

I live in the past, I can't forget, it has shaped me.

I have started to see a Counsellor, finally! Hooray! He's called David. I'm forty eight years old and I'm starting to see someone that basic common sense tells you that I should have been seeing before I was twenty six!

In truth, Claire and I should definitely have had counselling very soon after Mum's death. Seems like a good idea doesn't it after your Mum suffocates herself with a plastic bag on a Saturday night? Not an entirely normal weekend activity now is it?

Just a thought, a little thought Dad, a little tiny "thought-ette". If it's not too much trouble that is. Perhaps you had something to hide Dad, did you? Something that might have come out, that you wouldn't have wanted? Bet you did Dad, bet you did.

Bastard.

16 Manor Way

Can you feel the anger, can you? The anger that's inside me. Not difficult is it? That's because it's there. That's how I am. Nick, at forty eight. Nature or Nurture? Environmental determinism. A product of my past, just like you. No different.

I wake up several times each month dreaming that I am in 16 Manor Way, just after Dad has re-married, and I am trapped. I am compromised, put in very difficult situations, by the bitch wearing my Mother's watch. Dad has compromised me of course. And so I wake up, with a physical knot of tension and rage inside me. Sue is sound asleep, I go and check our wonderful children, and I can't get back to sleep for a long time.

That's how I am. Nick, adopted, son of an alcoholic mother. I wanted to write it all down, before I too die.

I hope that Katie and Russell, Claire and Graham's children, will one day read this story and come to know more about Claire, their Mum. I hope that you will see what a lovely woman your Mum was, even though she carried challenges with her.

I think she was born with some challenges as she arrived, and what was really tough, was that others were heaped onto her by those around her. These were people who should have done the complete opposite and who might have lessened your load Claire. People who were very close to you and who should have known better, but who failed you.

Let it be known that Claire was a good and popular person. A measure of that is that people wanted to see more of her, and that makes her a fine person. Claire was a person of integrity for me.

I hope she is with her Angels, I think she must be.

To my family, to Sue, Jack and Sophie, I say this. I hope that you will come to understand me better after you have read this story. I have told you some parts of it over the past few years, but here it is in its entirety, as best I can tell it. I am tired of it now. I need to move on to more healthy things.

When I withdraw into myself, as sometimes I do, it is because my past has come back to me in detail, and it will stay on my face for however long it stays. It usually likes to visit at times when you probably least want it – Christmas, Bank Holidays, big family gatherings. But perhaps now you see why.

It passes. I just ask that you give me time when it happens.

To Sue's family, her Mum Jan and her Dad Tony, and to her sister Katherine, I say this. I can see how you look at me sometimes. I can see that you think I'm odd, and yes I guess am.

"Guilty".

I am unusual, by virtue of the experiences that I have been asked to pass through. They are hardly very normal, but I am how I am as a result. They have shaped me. You may not like the shape always but please try to understand that I have a lot of sadness in me. I'll try better to integrate, really.

How different it might all have been. With just a little imagination, with the scales being tipped in a slightly different direction, what different outcomes might have been produced, what different people could have come out of our story.

This has been the story of Brian, Audrey, Claire and Nick Holbrook who lived together up until events in 1980 at No.16 Manor Way, Blackheath, London SE3 9EF.

Thank you for listening to it.

Nick, a boy adopted sometime in 1961.

www.ingramcontent.com/pod-product-compliance
Lightning Source LLC
Chambersburg PA
CBHW031206270326
41931CB00006B/439